# Paper Son

In the series

Asian American History and Culture,

edited by Sucheng Chan, David Palumbo-Liu, and Michael Omi

# Paper Son

## One Man's Story

Tung Pok Chin
*with* Winifred C. Chin

*With an Introduction by* K. Scott Wong

Temple University Press
PHILADELPHIA

Temple University Press, Philadelphia 19122
Copyright © 2000 by Temple University
All rights reserved
Published 2000
Printed in the United States of America

Library of Congress Cataloging-in-Publication Data

Chin, Tung Pok, d. 1988.
    Paper son : one man's story / Tung Pok Chin with Winifred C. Chin ; with
an introduction by K. Scott Wong.
        p. cm.—(Asian American history and culture)
    Includes bibliographical references.
    ISBN 1-56639-800-2 (cloth : alk. paper)
    ISBN 1-56639-801-0 (pbk. : alk. paper)
    1. Chin, Tung Pok, d. 1988. 2. Chinese Americans—Biography.
3. Immigrants—United States—Biography. 4. Illegal aliens—United States—
Biography. 5. Chinese—United States—Social Conditions—20th century.
6. Boston (Mass.)—Biography. 7. New York (N.Y.)—Biography. I. Chin,
Winifred C., 1952– . II. Title. III. Series.

E184.C5 P27 2000
973.049951—dc21                                    00-034347

In memory of
Dr. Ralph E. Pickett

# Contents

## Becoming American

*Photographs follow page 79*

# Preface

*Winifred C. Chin*

In June 1978, my father, Tung Pok Chin, a.k.a. Lai Bing Chan, was sixty-two years old and had just retired from laundry work to write his memoirs, *Paper Son*. He completed a rough draft in 1986 and gave it to me to edit. We worked together on editing the draft and translating his poems until he died in 1988 of cardiac arrest. In the years since then I have made some additions to the manuscript to fill in the domestic and international historical background to the key events in his life. Apart from these few additions, the story is as he left it when he died.

My father dedicated his book to his friend, Dr. Ralph E. Pickett, dean of the New York University School of Education when they met, who generously guided his self-education project and encouraged him to tell his life story.

# Introduction: Paper Lives

*K. Scott Wong*

When I first encountered Tung Pok Chin's *Paper Son*, I was immediately struck by his candor and his willingness to reflect on his life in an America that did not always welcome him and his fellow Chinese. Decades of exclusion laws and strained relations between China and the United States forced Chinese immigrants to assume false identities and construct fictional families, while at the same time do their best to sustain relationships with their real families and fulfill familial duties expected of them, both in China and America. Stated simply, the exclusion policy that prevailed from 1882 until 1943 limited the entry of Chinese to those of the "exempt classes" (that is, merchants, students, diplomats, and travelers), or those who could prove that one of their parents was a U.S. citizen. Thousands of men and far fewer women—no one knows how many people altogether—purchased documents that enabled them to begin new lives under false identities in this country. Many Chinese constructed and reconstructed their citizenship status, marital status, names, and personal pasts, depending on the trail of paper that created their immigrant identities and shaped their quest for official recognition as American citizens. Thus many Chinese Americans who entered the country from the mid-nineteenth through the mid-twentieth century led "paper lives" hidden in the shadows of exclusion. Chin's book opens the door on the daily life of a Chinese launderer on the East Coast and offers a glimpse of Chinese American history that has generally been kept within families, "paper" or otherwise. We have so few sources written from the perspective of Chinese immigrants that the publication of this memoir is especially welcome, as it enables us to document and understand the complexities of Chinese immigrant life in America.

For scholars and students, *Paper Son* is valuable because it documents a life during an era that is perhaps the least studied in Chinese American history, the 1930s through the mid-1970s. Set in Boston and New York, Chin's life story also serves to broaden our understanding of Chinese American history by shifting the focus of the exclusion process and its legacy from Angel Island and San Francisco's Chinatown to the Boston Immigration House and New York City. Chin's account not only reveals the details and strategy of how he conducted his "paper life"; it also puts human flesh to our skeletal knowledge of how paper sons lived their day-to-day lives during the Great Depression, World War II, and the McCarthy Era. To be sure, a number of good scholarly works document and analyze the rise of the anti-Chinese movement, the drive to exclusion, the intricacies of the paper son or "slot system," the rigorous interrogation process on Angel Island, the legal and social apparatuses that developed to enforce exclusion, and, to a lesser extent, the Chinese response to their greatly restricted lives in the United States.[1] Chin's memoir relates this information in a manner that is immediately accessible, warm, reflective, human, and insightful. No doubt his writing style reveals a great deal about his personality, but it also reminds us that much of our history of the exclusion era is faceless.

What do we know of that period? Chinese immigration to the United States (then as now) was driven by a desire for greater opportunity and shaped by a spectrum of forces. At the same time that the economy in southern China was failing, labor was being recruited to develop the American West, and this effort was augmented by American shipping firms' lucrative business of transporting labor and goods to various parts of the world. Certainly Chinese historical and cultural factors determined who would venture overseas in search of a reliable income. The transnational nature of Chinese migration and some Chinese emigrant families, as well as the draw of America as a place where riches could be made, all had a part in determining the character of Chinese immigration. Nothing, however, shaped the Chinese American experience as profoundly as the American immigration policy that effectively excluded most Chinese from entering the country from 1882 to 1943. The original Chinese Exclusion Act, passed in 1882, prohibited the immigration of Chinese laborers for ten years. This act was the first American immigration legislation to bar a particular group of people because of their race and class. Over time, this statute was renewed and strengthened, both in terms of occupations specified and geographical scope, until it was extended indefinitely in 1904. Not until 1943, when the United States and China were allies in World War II, was the bar lifted. And even then, the annual quota for Chinese entering the United States was set at a maximum of 105.[2]

For a variety of reasons, more Chinese men than women immigrated to the United States. Certain cultural factors enabled men to leave their wives in China while they worked in the United States, and some families decided that their best option would be for just the male to go abroad. But the exclusion policy also shaped Chinese immigrant communities in very direct ways. It stipulated that wives could not join their Chinese laborer husbands in America, thus limiting the Chinese female population in the United States and inhibiting the growth of families. In addition, many states passed anti-miscegenation laws that prevented Chinese from marrying white women, further reducing the natural growth of Chinese American families. The 1882 Exclusion Act also specified that Chinese immigrants were ineligible for naturalization. In a variety of ways, then, the structural and legal restrictions embodied in the Chinese Exclusion Acts ensured that the Chinese immigrant community was composed overwhelmingly of men and restricted them to certain occupations, with no hope of gaining the rights, privileges, responsibilities, and security of American citizenship. These barriers to full access to American life also profoundly affected the way immigrants and their descendants would come to view American society and the potential of their lives here.

Despite these barriers, Gold Mountain was still a powerful magnet for Chinese; some planned to send money home to improve their families' standard of living or to amass enough money so that they could return to a comfortable life in China; others intended to settle in America and create a Chinese American life. But plans do not always pan out. Some of those who intended to return to China after they had saved enough money ended up staying. Some who came to settle found their treatment so harsh and their possibilities so limited that they returned to China. In this regard, the Chinese resembled members of other immigrant groups who came to this country only to see their hopes dashed or their lives take an unexpected turn.

Once exclusion legislation took effect, Chinese immigration "went underground, and Chinese immigrants invented and employed a number of illegal immigration strategies that took advantage of loopholes in the exclusion laws themselves and in the government's enforcement of those laws."[3] The most common way around the law was to enter the country using fraudulent papers that declared the immigrant an American citizen or a citizen's son or grandson. Such claims to direct or derivative citizenship could facilitate legal entry into the country and confer citizenship on the immigrant. These papers, purchased in China, not only enabled one to establish one's citizenship status but also provided the information one needed to maintain a fictional relationship as a father, son, or grandson (far fewer Chinese women immigrated using this system). The immigrant memorized the information on his false papers in order to pass the interrogation by immigration officials at the American port of entry. The biggest break for those involved in paper son schemes came in 1906, when the San Francisco earthquake and the resulting fire destroyed a significant number of immigration and birth records. The loss of official records allowed many Chinese in the United States to launch successful claims to having been born here and to citizenship. Once their citizenship was established, they were able to create many "slots" for potential paper sons. As these claims became more numerous, the establishment of an immigration station on Angel Island (in San Francisco Bay) in 1910 became more significant. Between 1910 and 1940, the majority of Chinese emigrants attempting to enter the country were detained and interrogated there before being allowed to set foot in Gold Mountain. Some were detained on the island for months, even years, before their cases were settled. Once American immigration authorities became aware of the paper son system, the rigor of the interrogation intensified. Would-be immigrants needed to memorize increasingly detailed information, increasing the risk of mistakes and contradictions in their testimony and the likelihood that they would be denied entry and deported. Still, by the time Tung Pok Chin received his final visit from the FBI in 1959, "at least four or five generations of Taishanese were able to enter the U.S. through the network of paper sons."[4]

Among the few published accounts of paper sons and the interrogations on Angel Island and elsewhere, Chin's is the longest, most detailed, and most reflective.[5] He tells us, for instance, that he purchased a paper declaring him single, although he was married with two sons, because posing as someone unmarried required him to memorize fewer details. Like many other immigrants, he planned to return to China after making his fortune and had no thought of eventually bringing his family to this country. Throughout this memoir, he comments on the consequences of the exclusion policy, being a paper son, and sojourning patterns of many Chinese immigrants. His long separation from his wife and children in China led to his wife's infidelity and the eventual dissolution of their marriage. Even after he remarried in America, Chin remained fearful of being found out and kept certain details of his life hidden even from his new family.

Chin documents the indignities many Chinese Americans endured during the McCarthy era. Eager to catch illegal Chinese immigrants, especially any who might have supported the Communist regime in China, the FBI kept close surveillance on the Chinese American community. Chin's account of FBI agents' frequent visits to his laundry speaks to the tension felt throughout the community, especially among those with false papers. Chin was especially worried; in addition to his "paper" status, he frequently published his poetry and essays in the *China Daily News,* a Chinese-

language newspaper believed to have had communist leanings. During this period, the FBI and the Immigration and
Naturalization Service (INS) encouraged paper sons to confess their illegal status. In exchange for the information that
would expose the genealogies of "paper families," the INS
promised to assist informants in obtaining legal immigrant
status.[6] Although most of the people involved in the Confession Program did indeed become legal resident aliens or
naturalized citizens, the program created a variety of problems for many in the community. A confession implicated
not only the individual in question but others involved in
the system. Whole "paper families" would then be exposed,
often without the permission or knowledge of everyone
who would be implicated. Within the Chinese immigrant
community, relationships became strained and distrust of
the American government was widespread. Chin and his
wife chose not to confess and give up their citizenship status; anything could happen during the five-year wait
required before reapplying for citizenship. This anxiety certainly was not unique to the Chin household, and Chin's
memoir points to the dilemma many "paper families" must
have confronted.

   In addition to the information we gain about the everyday lives of paper sons in the Chinese American community, this memoir adds to what we know about the lives of
Chinese laundrymen. Chin's vivid descriptions of his nearly
twenty-hour work day, the cramped conditions of the laundry, the low pay, the social isolation, the brotherhood that
developed among laundry workers, and, for some launder-
ers, the possible sexual liaisons with young white women
recall Paul Siu's *The Chinese Laundryman: A Study of Social Isolation,* originally written as a doctoral dissertation in 1953
but not published until 1987.[7] Likewise, Chin's account of

seeking assistance from the Chinese Hand Laundry Alliance of New York reinforces the scholarly history of that organization written by Renqiu Yu.[8] Written as a personal testimony, *Paper Son* brings aspects of these academic histories to a much broader audience.

Chin's enlistment in the U.S. Navy during World War II also sheds light on an understudied period of Chinese American history. Some twelve to fifteen thousand Chinese Americans and Chinese immigrants served in the American armed forces during the war, including a substantial number of paper sons. Some chose to confess their "paper" status and were thus granted citizenship or the right to naturalize eventually, as was the case for B7, Chin's brother-in-law (B7 joined the service well after the war, but he was still allowed to confess his "paper" status and become eligible for naturalization). When Chin joined the navy, people of color could enlist only as mess attendants, also known as stewards' mates. Not until May 1942 could Chinese Americans enlist in the navy and hope to be more than waiters and cabin boys.

World War II opened up a new world of possibilities for Chinese Americans. For one thing, it enabled them to express their patriotism for the United States and their heartfelt nationalism for China. Serving in the American armed forces gave Chin the chance to claim a place in America, which reinforced his desire to build a life here. With the war also came increased social mobility and new opportunities for many Chinese immigrants and second-generation Chinese Americans. The GI Bill of Rights allowed many to gain a college education or make payments on houses outside of Chinatown. Significantly, the 1947 amendment to the War Brides Act of 1945 removed the act's original racial restrictions, allowing Chinese Americans to end long years of separation from their wives by bringing them to America or go to China to marry and return to the United States with their brides. For the first time in their history, Chinese Americans could establish families at a rate similar to that of other Americans.[9]

The publication of *Paper Son* is important because it documents the life of an individual Chinese immigrant who lived a rich and fascinating life and enriches our knowledge of Chinese American lives in the earlier half of this century. But it is also important because it gives voice to those thousands of paper sons who lived out their days in the shadow of exclusion, many of them carrying their secret to their graves. One consequence of their illegal status was that they could not openly express their feelings about being Chinese in America or about being American on paper only. Chin's book lets us into that world. Many of us may have paper sons in our families and not even know it. I did not find out that one of my grandfathers, also a launderer, was a paper son until more than sixty years after his death. In some ways, reading this book brought me closer to a grandfather I never knew. And I have a feeling that I will not be alone in this.

## Notes

1. The body of literature on the anti-Chinese movement is far too voluminous to cite here. Some of the most important studies are Mary R. Coolidge, *Chinese Immigration* (New York: Henry Holt and Company, 1909); Elmer C. Sandmeyer, *The Anti-Chinese Movement in California* (Urbana: University of Illinois Press, 1939); Stuart C. Miller, *The Unwelcome Immigrant: The American Image of the Chinese, 1875–1882* (Berkeley and Los Angeles: University of California Press, 1969); Alexander Saxton, *The Indispensable Enemy: Labor and the Anti-Chinese Movement in California* (Berkeley and Los Angeles: University of California Press, 1971); Sucheng Chan, ed., *Entry Denied: Exclusion and the Chinese Community in America, 1882–1943* (Philadelphia: Temple University Press, 1991); Charles J. McClain, *In Search of Equality: The Chinese Struggle against Dis-*

*crimination in Nineteenth-Century America* (Berkeley and Los Angeles: University of California Press, 1994); Lucy E. Salyer, *Laws Harsh as Tigers: Chinese Immigrants and the Shaping of Modern Immigration Law* (Chapel Hill: University of North Carolina Press, 1995); and Andrew Gyory, *Closing the Gate: Race, Politics, and the Chinese Exclusion Act* (Chapel Hill: University of North Carolina Press, 1998). For a collection of essays focusing on the Chinese immigrant and the Chinese American response to exclusion, see K. Scott Wong and Sucheng Chan, eds., *Claiming America: Constructing Chinese American Identities during the Exclusion Era* (Philadelphia: Temple University Press, 1998).

2. The evolution of these laws can be traced in 22 U.S. Statutes at Large 58–61; 25 U.S. Statutes at Large 476–479; 27 U.S. Statutes at Large 25–26; 28 U.S. Statutes at Large 1210–1212; 32 U.S. Statutes at Large 176–177; 33 U.S. Statutes at Large 428; and 43 U.S. Statutes at Large 153–169.

3. Erika Lee, "At America's Gates: Chinese Immigration During the Exclusion Era, 1882–1943" (Ph.D. diss., University of California, Berkeley, 1998), pp. 229–30.

4. Madeline Hsu, " 'Living Abroad and Faring Well': Migration and Transnationalism in Taishan County, Guangdong 1904–1939" (Ph.D diss., Yale University, 1996), p. 120.

5. See Him Mark Lai, Genny Lim, and Judy Yung, *Island: Poetry and History of Chinese Immigrants on Angel Island, 1910–1940* (Seattle: University of Washington Press, 1991. Originally published by San Francisco: HOC DOI, 1980). Erika Lee's dissertation also makes extensive use of the interviews and immigration records from Angel Island.

6. See Mai M. Ngai, "Legacies of Exclusion: Illegal Chinese Immigrants during the Cold War Years," Journal of American Ethnic History 18:1 (fall 1998): 3–35.

7. See Paul C. P. Siu, *The Chinese Laundryman: A Study of Social Isolation,* ed. John Kuo Wei Tchen (New York: New York University Press, 1987).

8. See Renqiu Yu, *To Save China, To Save Ourselves: The Chinese Hand Laundry Alliance of New York* (Philadelphia: Temple University Press, 1992).

9. For a study of the impact of World War II on Chinese Americans, see K. Scott Wong, "War Comes to Chinatown: Social Transformation and the Chinese of California," in *The Way We Really Were: The Golden State in the Second Great War,* ed. Roger Lotchin (Urbana: University of Illinois Press, 2000).

# Paper Son

# Prologue

Toward the end of the nineteenth century, United States laws did not extend immigration privileges to Chinese people. The Chinese Exclusion Act of 1882 barred the immigration of Chinese laborers for the next ten years, and in the ensuing years a series of acts severely limited Chinese immigration and naturalization. It was not until 1943 that the acts were repealed, an annual immigration quota was set, and naturalization privileges were granted to the Chinese.

During the time that Chinese were excluded, immigrants entered the United States by purchasing a "paper" designating them as the sons or daughters of Chinese Americans. The first Chinese Americans were probably the children of the 1850s Chinese railroad workers out west, but no one knows for sure. When this first generation of American-born Chinese later visited China, they married, returned to the United States, and in due time reported that they had left children behind in the motherland. The United States government would issue a paper allowing these "children" to immigrate, though whether or not they ever existed is another story. For the owners of these papers sold them to agents in the Chinese black market, who in turn sold them to people seeking to come to America as the children of natives. Each paper cost $100 U.S. for each year of the child's age, payable before departure, or, more commonly, to be worked off upon arrival.

I arrived in Boston as a "paper son" in 1934, at the age of nineteen. After three days of interrogation at the Immigration House, having satisfactorily answered all questions regarding my "father," answers I had memorized months before, I emerged a United States citizen, the son of a native, ready to begin my life anew in "Gold Mountain," the United States of America.

# The Early Years

# Gold Mountain

When I was a child sixty years ago, "Gold Mountain" was a household word in Tai-shan County, the least productive district in the entire Guangdong Province of southern China. But ironically it was financially the richest, because more than half its population of 1 million received U.S. dollars for their daily living expenses.

"My husband goes to Gold Mountain," women use to brag proudly. Gold Mountain, of course, meant the United States of America, where husbands worked long days and nights in restaurants and laundries to enable their families back home to build huge and lofty houses and hire maidservants to show that they were well off. When U.S. dollars were cut off during the Japanese invasion just before World War II, much of the population died helplessly from starvation.

The following incident is still deeply rooted in my memory: In my village sixty years ago, a poor woman, whose husband went abroad and never returned or sent money home, sold her only teenage daughter for the sum of $10 to a Gold Mountain wife. Within a short time the girl ran away with some money and returned to her mother. The next day her mistress raised a posse of women, all dressed in their Sunday best, with gold bracelets, gold earrings, and gold rings set with precious stones, to retrieve the girl. What displays of wealth! As a six-year-old boy, seeing the way they came and hearing their voices, I was awed and frightened. The smell of perfume that wafted from their beautiful dresses made the farm wives envious with startling eyes.

However, there was one thing that farm wives never understood: the lives of grass widows, women who were divorced or separated from their husbands. Some liked living as grass widows and some did not. Some would not swap their husbands for all the gold in the United States.

There was a story told among the Chinese laundry men here in these United States of America about a father-and-son team that entered the country illegally. After spending some long years here, the father retired and returned to the motherland to enjoy his last days on the soil where he was born. One day as the old man was chatting with the country folk under the shaded trees, his grandson called to him to come to supper. Just as he sat down at the table and was ready to be served, the boy's mother grumbled at him, "You old pig, why didn't you bring along your son? Why just come back by yourself?" Taking this to heart the old man did his best to persuade his son to return home. When the son finally returned, the old man said sourly to his daughter-in-law, "My daughter-in-law, I now hand back your husband to you. You can now satiate your upper mouth as well as your lower mouth. Let us, if you don't mind, share poverty together." The young woman retorted bitterly, "Father-in-law, I wouldn't trade my husband for all the American dollars in the world."

Yes, to live as a grass widow is unhealthy, you got to know that. It is unfair, you got to realize it. I don't blame that woman one bit for her complaint.

The myth of Gold Mountain, no matter what perspective you take, is still alive today. It has its attractions, you know. Some of the early American-born Chinese, taking advantage of their circumstances, would travel to-and-fro between the two countries every few years so that they could report having some sons and daughters by the time they came back to the United States. One of my villagers, who claimed to be American-born, sold papers for eight nonexistent sons besides his own two sons produced by his concubine, when his big fat wife produced only two daughters!

As you see, the "paper" trade was a very lucrative business, and one could accumulate a small fortune very quickly if one did not mind a bad reputation. A certain Mr. Lee sold a paper daughter for $10,000, which she paid back by whoring on Oxford Street in Boston. On the right side of the whorehouse was a Chinese Confucian school and on its left a missionary church operated by a few aged American ladies who were helped to Sunday School by a Chinese laundry man. When the ladies disapproved of his marrying the young white girl who assisted him at his laundry, he left for San Francisco and in 1937 became president of the powerful Hip Sing Tong.

Frequent visitors to the one-woman whorehouse used to stand on line Sunday mornings from the second floor down to the sidewalk, each patiently awaiting his turn. One day a youth was waiting on line, while his father was on his way to the same spot. "Hey, your son is in there," somebody called to warn him. "I am going to give him moral instruction," the father jokingly replied and went on his way.

One of the richest men in New York's Chinatown made a fortune by putting his concubine into this business. When his first cousin came from Boston for a visit and tried to share her bed with her, she refused. "No, you are my husband's cousin. It can't be done," she said, and would not give in. "It is a disgrace. A disgrace to our ancestors," my friend said. "And she invited me to join her picnic party at Coney Island, bringing with her some homemade pastries. I wouldn't dare to eat them. Those dicks—she washes them with her own hands after each transaction!" He made a face and I laughed to my heart's content.

But not all Gold Mountain men arrive in the United States to live forever a lonely existence separated from their families back home. There is the story of a young man in the early 1930s who returned home at the first opportunity. A former classmate of mine in China, he won $2,000 one night playing fan-tan in a gambling house in New York's Chinatown.[1] Anxious to be reunited with his wife from whom he had parted about a year before, he demanded the "son of native" paper that was in his father's safekeeping.

"You have not paid the paper son money yet. Why are you in such a hurry to go back home?" his father scolded. But his love for his young wife overcame his duties as a son. When his father refused a second and third time to turn over the paper, a fight broke out between the two. The father, being neither as strong nor as tall as the son, naturally lost. He was terribly beaten, with nose bloodied, head injured, and shirt torn to shreds.

The son finally ran off to the San Francisco Immigration House to report the loss of this paper in the 1906 earthquake and obtained a new one there. He returned to China and never again entertained the thought of leaving. The father, meanwhile, sent the torn and bloodstained shirt to his own wife of thirty years, still living in China, cried abandonment by their son, and brought her over instead by purchasing a paper daughter's contract for her. Upon retirement he sold his laundry in Sheepshead Bay in Brooklyn and bought a small boat so that he and his wife could enjoy their golden years in travel!

[1] Fan-tan is a game in which the dealer, or banker, divides a pile of flat beads or beans into fours and players bet on what number will be left at the end of the count. It is played on a rectangle the size of a ping-pong table. A square is drawn in the center, and the lower right-hand corner is "1," the upper right "2," the upper left "3," and the lower left "4." A bet placed on any one of the four corners wins one to three. A bet placed between any two corners wins one to one. To play, the dealer takes a handful of flat beads and places them on the table, covering them with a lid. The players then place their bets. After all bets are placed, the dealer lifts the lid with a flat bamboo stick and removes fours beads at a time, until the last remaining beads number 1, 2, 3, or 4. That is the winning number and corner. Since the game is played on four corners of a square, the slang expression for playing fan-tan is "to attack the square city."

# My Village

My village was and probably still is the size of a football field, with fewer than fifty families. Sha-tou Ch'uen, the poorest of the poor, literally means, "Sand Head village." It is a village built at the head of a patch of fine sand. Sixty odd years ago a five-year-old boy, sick with fever, barefoot, and naked from the waist up, with only a pair of old patched pajama-like pants on, bought two cakes of salted bean curd with a penny and carried them away in a wooden rice bowl. On his way home from the north end of the village to the south, a ten-year-old boy accosted him, saying, "You want some sugar?" and he picked some dirt up off the ground and deposited it into his bowl. The sick boy finally had to get salt water to wash down his rice. This is a true story—I saw it myself. Survival was tough then; even the poor Chinese villagers of today are much better fed than the people of sixty years ago.

Tai-shan County was unique among the counties of Guangdong Province. Before World War II more than half the heads of households in Tai-shan villages made their living in either the United States or Cuba. My village was no exception, but only a few made enough to send money home. Wives back home had to toil alone for their daily bread. Much worse, they had to live alone. Now, in such a small community everyone's business becomes everyone else's, especially concerning immoral conduct. One woman in her late twenties, having no children, her husband far away in another land, had a rendezvous with a young man in her own house and got caught in the act at midnight. The men of the village were ready to put her into a bamboo cage and drown her. I heard the woman cry, "Father-in-law, do you want me?" And I heard the old man reply, "No. I don't want you anymore." She was driven away the very same night but the young man was freed unharmed.

To the east, my village had a five-foot cement wall topped with barbed wire. The other three sides were planted with bamboo several feet thick. One summer night a group of bandits cut a big hole in the northwest corner and raided the village, wounding a few and carrying away sixteen captives, young and old, women and men. Each carried a ransom of anywhere from $200 to $2,000 Hong Kong. One Gold Mountain man who lived and owned a restaurant in New York paid $2,000 to get his four-year-old daughter out but would not redeem his father. The restaurant owner, you see, was only a "paper" son, not a son by birthright. That was in 1923.

Seeing that there was no way to regain his freedom, the helpless and pitifully aged father tried to escape from the bandits' well-fortified mountain hideout just ten miles from my village, but he was recaptured and forced to gather green grass every day and to sleep over it at night. Eventually he was beaten to death by the bandits with rifle butts and his body was finally redeemed for $500 Hong Kong. People say it was all his old woman's fault: She wanted to revenge herself and would not let the so-called "son" redeem the father because the old man himself had stayed more than forty years in the United States, leaving the woman barren and uncultivated to sleep alone during her young flowering years. What a pity!

One of the leaders of the bandits, who numbered in the hundreds, was a woman nicknamed "Single-eyed Eagle."

Children used to stop crying right away when mothers mentioned her name. Single-eyed Eagle was plain, fat, short, and blind in one eye. Her first husband was making his living abroad and never sent her a damn penny. As a result she had to keep herself alive by cutting wood in the mountains. One day she was captured by the bandits. Villagers passed their hats around to collect a ransom for her. She didn't stay long in the village though. She ran back to the hideout to cast her lot with the bandits. Single-eyed Eagle could shoot straight simultaneously with both hands and never miss her targets within one hundred yards! Even the bandits were really "sons of guns." One of our village night watchmen struck a match one night to light the searchlight and was immediately shot on the fingertip from two hundred feet away!

One year later the bandits were captured by government troops. Single-eyed Eagle was chained together with her handsome three-year-old son and her second husband, the chief of the bandits. They were executed, but some people say that the governor secretly released the husband after another prisoner was masked and substituted for him just before the execution. You see, the governor and the bandit chief were of the same family name, and the chief, it was rumored, had once done the governor a great favor in childhood.

# A Gold Mountain Man

I arrived in the United States in Boston in 1934 at the age of nineteen. I had purchased my "paper," designating me the son of an American native, on the Chinese black market, and would automatically become a United States citizen upon verification of the facts. For months before leaving China I studied these "facts": my paper name, my paper father's name, my paper mother's name, my age, their ages, my place of birth, their places of birth, their occupations, and so on.

This was not easy. I had to completely block out my real and immediate family: my parents who raised me and arranged a marriage for me at the age of thirteen, my wife, my two young sons, aged four and five at the time of my arrival in Boston, and all else that related to them. One slip during the interrogation and I would be sent back on the next boat to China! And the methods they used were tricky. Questions were asked nonstop, one after another under a glaring light, and the key questions were repeated over and over again to catch any inconsistencies. And of course they expected quick answers—who would not know his own parents' names at the snap of a finger? Luckily, my paper was fairly simple; it was for a single person with no family or obligations. This meant that there was less to memorize and less possibility of a slipup. I could have purchased a paper for a married man with two sons, but that would have meant more names and dates to memorize. Opting for a single-person paper meant that I could not bring my sons over to the United States, but that was not my objective. Like all other Gold Mountain dreamers, I wanted to make my fortune and return home a wealthy and envied man.

My real father, already in Gold Mountain as a paper son himself, made my passage to America possible. He informed me of the availability of this particular paper and then, in a manner befitting a spy novel, I obtained it from the "agent" in my village. My father also managed to borrow enough money from a distant cousin to finance my trip. My paper, at a cost of $100 for each year recorded—that is, each year of my age—cost me $2,000 with fee, excluding transportation. This I was able to purchase on credit and would repay when I arrived and found work.

Late in the summer of 1934, after three days of intensive interrogation in a dingy little room at the Boston Immigration House, I walked away a United States citizen. I was now a Gold Mountain man and had broken the bonds of poverty that marked the Sha-tou villagers! Yet I knew that I had a long way to go before I could call myself a free man, for I was overburdened with debt. I was excited, though, eager, and most of all determined. I learned to iron shirts and within two months was hired out in Providence, Rhode Island, at $8 a week.

Mr. Chin was my first employer.

"How long have you been here, Uncle Chin?"

"Forty years," he said.

"And you have never gone back to see the old woman?"

"What is the use of seeing the old woman?" he retorted. "I have a son there, he got married and got me grandsons. I bought acres of rice fields, built a new house, and now I send money home to bring up all the grandchildren." He enumerated them proudly. As I sat listening to him, I felt sad for him—and for myself and my future. I wondered if this would be my fate, too. For like everyone else in my village, I had visions of someday returning home in grandeur.

Uncle Chin was content, however. He had a C.O.D. white girl (prostitute) to supply what he needed. And indeed, while we were talking, a smiling young face appeared at the doorway.

"Charlie, you want to see me?" asked the girl. She came in without waiting for an answer, but Uncle Chin sent her away without completing his transaction.

"Here," he handed her two quarters, "go away." He smiled stealthily as he tightened up his greasy white cotton apron to prepare for work. "I don't do anything with her," he turned to me, feeling a little embarrassed.

Uncle Chin was very stingy. During the two weeks that I worked for him, what we ate were pork bellies cooked with shrimp sauce and two bowls of rice. He kept a glass jar of bean curds underneath the stack of starch crates that were covered up with an old unclaimed sheet to serve as a dining table. During the morning and night meals he would eat his bowl of rice. Then he took out the jar from underneath the crates, opened it, and with his pair of soiled chopsticks, picked out a piece of bean curd and deposited it into his rice bowl. The cost of one piece of bean curd was less than a penny, but he never offered me one. I never got enough to eat when I worked for Uncle Chin.

After completing my second week with him I returned to Boston and got a new job with Uncle Lee in Somerville at $15 a week. The fall weather was setting in, and I, being from the southernmost tip of China, was not prepared for the weather changes of the northeastern United States.

"You have no overcoat in this kind of weather?" Lee asked me.

"No. I have no money to afford one," I said.

"I lend you mine," he said plainly. When I put on the coat its length reached my ankles and the sleeves covered my fingertips. I wore his coat every Sunday for the entire fall and winter.

Uncle Lee was an easygoing man. By the time I met him, he had already spent thirty years here and was well established in his business. He was a heavy gambler, though. One Sunday night he lost all his savings in a Chinatown gambling house and rushed back to the laundry by taxi, asking me for a loan of $70. But his lucky star was not with him. I could not help him. It was not long, however, before I joined him in this sinful pastime. Uncle Lee was talkative, too, and his favorite subject was women. When he reached his favorite part of a story he even left the iron on the shirt that he was pressing, gesturing with both hands and laughing heartily.

"Hey, perhaps you were the one my wife asked if I wanted to buy," he said curiously.

"Was it your village that had a coed school, and there was a big tree at the end of the village—and a woman with bound feet?" I asked.

"It was," he replied.

"She kept me for some time and then sent me back at last to the fat lady who managed to sell me. Then finally I was resold to the Lai family who raised me as their own."

"Yes. I sent a letter. Told her to buy an older one, old enough to go to bed with her. Then she stopped that silly idea," he said. "I don't care if she fools around with somebody as long as she produces no bastard. That's a bad name. I mean, she should have the same rights as I do here," he laughed again. "Anyway, how was it that you were sold?"

"I was carried away by a small group of bandits on a pitch dark night from a small farm. The bandits tied my mother with my two-year-old sister on her back around the branch of a big papaya tree, and one of the bandits put me on his back. I heard my mother and sister screaming all the way." It's a sad story, but a common one in a China then overrun by warlords.

Uncle Lee's wife turned out to be a distant cousin, the niece of my father's sister. She was poor all her life. On the rainy days water dripped everywhere from the roof, and she could hardly find a dry spot to sleep on. But she was happy and never complained of poverty. She was a firstborn. Her mother cast her away in a bamboo basket the very moment she was born, but her grandmother took her back and named her "Liu-hsin," which means "keep [the] new[born]."

Oh, how the Chinese used to hate girls. They still do, especially now that the motto in China is "one child per family." Stories are often heard of parents abandoning their firstborn girls, or drowning them, most often in the countryside. It is a sad lot indeed to be born a girl in China.

Uncle Lee and I quickly became the best of friends. We talked about almost everything. He was a very knowledgeable man in general, and knowledgeable too of the unspoken laws that rule Chinese life here in America. It was thanks to Uncle Lee that I realized I had to do something for myself or forever remain the pawn of those to whom I was now paying my debts. As we relaxed one evening after dinner, he made a confession in confidence to me.

"You know," he said, "I almost killed your father once. He belongs to On Leung Tong and I to Hip Sing Tong. And no one is closer related than the members of the same tong. They call themselves each other's hands and feet. During a tong war even brothers would not see each other if each belonged to opposing tongs, just to avoid a possible confrontation."

He told me the heroic stories of the hatchet men and the bounty hunters of both tongs, Chinese organized crime gangs, which I found very fascinating. But finally my curiosity could not be contained.

"How were tongs organized in the first place?" I asked.

"Well, it is commonly said back home, 'Guangdong Chin, and Worldwide Lee.' In other words there are more people in Guangdong Province with the surname Chin [Chen or Chan in other dialects] than any other name, but more people in the world with the surname Lee.

"Now people with big family names here in Boston do the same thing as they do in China when the big villages oppress the smaller ones, or when the big clans in the same village bully the smaller clans—they take the law into their own hands. So people with small family names here in Boston joined hands together and formed the On Leung Tong, which means 'Organization to Pacify the Good.' Hip Sing Tong, which means 'Organization United to Win,' was formed by other family name members. But you know, to pay the devil its due credit, a tong is not too bad in some ways."

As I became more familiar with life in the Chinese community here, I came to realize the power and influence of the tongs. They are controlled by powerful business interests in and around the Chinatown community. Each has its own territory on which others cannot trespass. Within these territories, "protection fees" are extracted from commercial establishments and paid to the controlling tong. Nonpayment can bring severe economic and physical penalties. Many merchants and residents in Chinatown believe even today that these fees are partially used for police payoffs to protect organized gambling and Mafia-like activities, but these are only whispered of. In the past as today, youth groups, especially minors, are most often used for collecting fees, because if arrested and charged they are only tried as juveniles.

I worked for Uncle Lee for nearly half a year, through the summer of 1935. I ate good food at his laundry and got $15 in weekly wages. I was also learning a lot more about life in Gold Mountain.

One Sunday my father called me and asked me to take over his laundry. At age fifty-seven, he was ill. When I got to the laundry I found a loaded .38 caliber pistol inside a teapot hidden in a bamboo basket. It was covered with a soiled napkin, but ready to be fired at any time.

"Why do you keep a pistol here?" I asked.

"In case I have to use it in a tong war."

"For what reason? Mr. Lee tried to kill you?"

"He was a hatchet man of Hip Sing Tong, and I am a member of On Leung Tong. A hatchet man is a gunman who takes prizes on members of the opposing tong during a war. There is a reward of $500, and Lee Heung, the tally man, announced publicly in Chinatown that he wanted me killed. But he wouldn't dare try."

"Yes. He told me that once."

"He would never make it. I would kill him first the moment he stepped foot into this laundry," he said confidently.

"No," I replied. "He just didn't want to. If he did, it would be as easy as drawing a match from his coat pocket. He could have slipped a splinter of wood into the keyhole here and waited for you to come back at night, and then shot you in the back in cold blood while you tried to unlock the door. He didn't do it because you and he are distantly related."

My father was speechless as I related to him my conversation with Uncle Lee.

# Between Father and Son

My father's laundry was located at 87 Chelsea Street in Charlestown, Massachusetts. The store was very small, about ten feet by fifteen feet. One-third of the space was used as a drying room, and in this space stood a sink, a portable gas range, and a coal stove for drying shirts. On the ceiling were some wires attached at each end to two wooden two-by-fours nailed to the wall; the wires were used for hanging shirts. In the extreme left corner was a stairway that led to the basement, where a ton of coal was stored in the corner to the right; the toilet was to the left. He slept at night on a board, two feet by six feet, suspended by heavy wire from the ceiling—a sort of wooden hammock! I slept in the drying room on a wooden board positioned on top of two wooden horses that we used as stepladders when hanging shirts from the ceiling. The wallpaper was blackened and peeling from the moisture in the air. The chief reason why laundry men could afford to go back to the homeland once every few years was that they were able to save money on rent and transportation by living in their laundries.

Now, business for this particular laundry, which was near a navy yard, had been good. But an old friend of my father's with a big family opened a laundry two blocks away at the top of Bunker Hill, and my father's business soon fell off—in fact, it dwindled to almost nothing. When people asked this old friend why he had to open a laundry so close to his good friend and "break his rice bowl," he replied,

"This is Gold Mountain. I have the freedom to do business wherever I choose!" His friend was right. He had learned the secrets of free enterprise.

"The paper I arranged for your passage to the United States cost $2,000; the boat and train expenses were about another $400. That is a total of $2,400. Have you paid back any money to Yu Nap?" my father inquired the first night we met at his laundry. "After all, you have come to the United States nearly a year ago now."

Yu Nap is the second son of my father's third brother. He came to this country in his early twenties, first as a paper son, but gave the wrong answer at Immigration and broke the contract. He returned one year later as the son of a merchant, which meant that he had the right to come in once but not to reenter if for any reason he left the country. He tried to marry in the United States, but his mother picked a girl for him in China and told him that if he did not come home, she would hang herself. He finally did return, but his father-in-law managed to find him another paper son contract, for one old enough not to be inducted into the army in the event of another world war.

"I have not and cannot pay him anything yet. You know that I make only $15 a week [which was top pay for hired help in the laundry business in 1935], and when I come out to Chinatown on Sundays you always demand half of it as gambling money. As for the rest of the money, I have a family back home to support. I don't even have money to buy a winter coat. This ragged coat was given to me, worn out to the sleeves, by Cousin Sing Tu when he asked and discovered I had none. Before this, I only borrowed Uncle Lee's.

"You know, as a hired help to Uncle Lee I ate good food and earned $15 a week. Why do you call me back here when you have only twenty some odd dollars of business yourself? You have come to the United States more than ten years now, and you have not contributed a penny toward this paper. To pay back all this debt I have to work fifteen or more years," I said.

"Oh, don't worry. You don't have to pay Yu Nap the whole amount before going home for a visit. I want you to know that I did my best to get you here. In the first place Yu Nap wanted to get his brother here. When he came and asked me for my opinion, I told him that I am too old and could not help him in any way. So he changed his mind and got a paper suitable for your age. It costs $100 for each year of your age. It wasn't stated in the paper either that you were married and have two sons because it would cost even more. Besides, there would be more questions to answer in the paper. As for this laundry, I know it is a financial loss to you, but I paid $1,500 for it. It is my hope that business will pick up again some day. You've got to learn that to be a one-penny boss is better than to be a two-penny hire-out," he said. He was right in this sense, and so for the time being I remained at my father's laundry, my own boss.

# Everybody for Himself

Sing Tu and Sing Suey were brothers. Their father and my father were second cousins. So in name we were cousins. But in fact I was somewhat of an alien to them. I was, after all, a child kidnapped and sold to the Lai household, not a true relation.

In Sha-tou village we built two houses under one roof. Their side of this complex had one kitchen and one bedroom and was the first house in the first lane. My side occupied the second lane. Between the houses was an open space and a hall where the ancestral tablets were placed, covered by the roof that joined the two structures.

Sing Suey was in his teens when his father died, and his elder brother, Sing Tu (who had already come to the United States), sent him to live at Pui Ching Middle School in Canton, one of the finest institutions in the province. After graduating he became editor of the fiction column of a nationalist newspaper in Hong Kong. Soon afterward, he too came to the United States. He was not married at the time, but his brother bought him a paper at the cheap rate of $1,200 and reported that he was. For this, Sing Tu forgave his brother the entire debt, the cost of the paper as well as the fare for boat and train. When Sing Suey came to the United States and learned the ropes of the laundry trade, Sing Tu left the laundry in his care and returned to Hong Kong for two years.

Now, Sing Suey made about $50 a week at his brother's laundry in 1935. I could not make even $5 a week in my father's, so I sold the business for the total sum of $200. All I really got was $110 in this transaction, which took place at the office of the Chinese Consolidated Benevolent Association, Chinatown's equivalent of City Hall. The other $90 was shared proportionately by my father's debtors. He was $2,400 in debt—all from gambling! The buyer, a certain Mr. Lee, did me the favor at his own suggestion of reporting the selling price as only $100. Thus I got $10 for the deposit of the selling price, and he secretly gave me the other $100 before the official transaction.

After selling the laundry, I started working for Sing Suey at $15 a week. With this $15 I had to buy necessities for my father every Sunday when I visited him in the hospital. My father had asked me to raise $400 for his final return to Hong Kong, so I asked Sing Suey to lend me $50 and told him that he could deduct the amount from my wages, but he refused.

"But when we were in Hong Kong we talked and agreed that we should stick together and help each other out in the United States," I said.

"Life is different here. Don't you see the American people? When a group of friends go to a movie everybody pays for himself; there is no such thing as the Chinese custom of rushing ahead to pay for the others. Here, everybody is for himself," he replied.

"But my father is your uncle, and I am working for you; you can deduct it in a few weeks." But he would not listen to me.

"Who knows if one gets the money today that he will not fly away tomorrow with his wallet safely tucked in his pocket? Men's hearts are full of greed. You know now that we must work very hard in Gold Mountain to get even our basic necessities. How shall I get my money back if that hap-

pens?" Sing Suey was afraid I would abandon my
run away for $50!

Upon hearing my words in his hospital bed _
Plain, a neighborhood of Boston, my father raised his weak-
ened body to a sitting position, his voice trembling, and
asked, "Why are you still working for him? Why don't you
quit and find a job somewhere else? As long as you have the
will to work you won't die of starvation." He was right, and
so I left to seek my own fate.

My father was barely literate, but when he was ready to
accept the reunion call of his forefathers from the other
world, he warned me: "Don't join On Leung Tong; don't
bring your sons to the United States; don't gamble." The
Philosopher T'sang said: "When a man is about to die, his
word is good." I agree.

My mother, herself a beauty and twelve years my
father's junior, also could barely read or write. It didn't matter much for an old-fashioned girl anyway, because Confucius said: "For a girl, having no education is a virtue." I
remember as a child how my mother used to moan and
murmur to herself, mostly at night, "Oh, when he goes
away, he goes eight or ten years. When he comes back he
stays only six months and then flies away again like a bird,
just like a bird."

I couldn't understand this woeful situation as a boy of
seven. No, not until I came of age and knew of the relationship between husband and wife could I feel her sorrow.
She was most unfortunate to marry a man with whom she
shared a common fate but over whom she had little control.
She was widowed at age forty-seven, having spent only
eighteen months as a wife to her husband in twenty-five
years of marriage.

As soon as my father was buried and I was ready to leave Boston for New York, an old friend of his advised me, "You are young. There is a whole world ahead of you. You must remain here for the period of mourning after the funeral." So I did, and he introduced me to Mr. Yung.

Mr. Yung was my employer during the last two weeks of my stay in Boston. Working for him was truly an eye opener. He was undoubtedly a successful businessman. In 1935 he was already equipped with shirt pressing machines that I was later to encounter at the United States naval base at Agentia, Newfoundland, in 1942. Besides himself he employed five men, and he himself worked harder than any of the others. When he carried a big laundry bag full of nurses' uniforms on his back and delivered them to the nearby hospital, he scampered all the way there, losing no time at all. His income was probably more than ten times that of any other individual laundry owner.

Our workday lasted from seven o'clock in the morning until two o'clock the next morning, day in and day out, six days a week. We ate supper at two o'clock in the morning and slept at two-thirty. We had only four and one-half hours of sleep daily. But he was a man of his word. He said he would treat us well, and he did. A Confucian gentleman of the highest order, he promised me $15 a week but paid me $18 instead. He tried very hard to retain me at the end of the month, but my mind was set on making a new start.

"I know Ming Wai, your cousin. He promises to help you in New York, but don't consider it seriously until money is in your hands. You should stay here with me," he said. He was right too, for at that time $18 a week for a hire-out in the laundry business was top pay.

"My father spoke the same words," I told him, "but I have to try my luck. I have a family of four to feed and a paper son's debt to pay."

That very night I packed my bags for New York. I did not keep contact with Mr. Yung, although he was never far from my thoughts. Nor would that be the last that I would hear of him. Twenty some odd years later, I met Mr. Yung's older cousin in a grocery store in New York City's Chinatown. When I asked about Mr. Yung, he just shook his head sadly.

"What happened to him?"

"Big Brother," he told me, "he spent all of his savings on his two sons and he is now poor like a dog, living alone in the Yung's Club Room in Boston. His older son, for whom he paid room and board at Harvard, studied to be a doctor of philosophy; his younger son, having the same amenities at Ch'ing Hua University in Peking, finally came to Harvard also. He again paid for everything. After the war Yung bought each of them a one-family house on Long Island and kept nothing for his old age. 'Raise sons to ward against old age,' so the Chinese say. But instead, no one took him in. So he took turns staying at each son's house. At last he got fed up and gathered his handful of clothing in a bag and said angrily, 'I shall go back to Boston. I don't care if the two of you leave me to die of starvation.' He is poor now, like an old dog."

I don't know about it nowadays, but the old dogs of China used to eat the excrement of human beings left on the roadside, especially that left by the babies. The mothers would spread their babies' legs apart, lift up their heels from the ground and set them to soil on the roadside. When the baby was through, a wandering dog was sure to come and lap it clean. If there were two dogs at the same time they would even fight over it.

The old-fashioned and more traditional Chinese used to think that they had a better family system than Western society, and many Westerners tend to agree. They think that the Confucian doctrines of the past two thousand years are so deeply rooted in our minds and that the principles of filial piety have so permeated society, high and low alike, that no forces could ever break the bonds of our closely knit families. That may have been true back in the old country, but things are different in the New World. Uproot these two Yung brothers from their homes in China, plant them in Gold Mountain with the best education an American university can offer, grant them the freedom of mobility of which American society boasts, and the ties between father and son, and all the studies of filial piety, do not stand a chance.

Many Chinese who have come to Gold Mountain seeking a better way of life for themselves and their families share a similar fate. Some say it is the American family system, small and private, that changes the new generation, and the older generation is too slow to adapt to the newer way of life. Gone is the custom of living under one roof, one extended family, relying on one's sons to plow one plot of land for security in old age. Here, one must keep one's savings against old age, as the Americans do. But then again, the overwhelming debts that the new immigrant is constantly confronted with adds unforeseen pressure on the formerly and otherwise filial son. Children have their own families to care for and can no longer look after their parents as they would have in China. Unfortunately it is the older generation that suffers, because the future belongs to the young.

# Fighting Chinese City Hall

In 1935 New York's Chinatown was very small. Three blocks on Mott Street between Canal Street and Chatham Square and two blocks on Bayard Street were under the influence of On Leung Tong; two blocks on Pell and Doyer Streets were controlled by Hip Sing Tong. Those who lived on Mott Street were often warned by the older generation not to set foot onto Pell Street for fear of getting killed in a gang war. One's address alone was enough to link a person to one side or the other in times of violence! These were what the older generation often spoke of as "spheres of influence," territories that "belonged" to a given tong, and no one could interfere with that area in gambling or other interests. You see, gambling was big business in Chinatown in the 1930s, and it still is.

In that era, weekdays in Chinatown were dead quiet—just like a cemetery, especially in the mornings before eleven o'clock. Even Sundays were quiet. With the exception of business on the ground floors, all upstairs floors were occupied by *kung shih fang*, little club rooms where members of the same family name gathered together to play mahjong or discuss family business. Very few people walked the streets, a marked contrast to today.

Members of the kung shih fang were a simple lot, mostly laundry men by occupation, and politics did not concern them. Many of the older generation did not read or write; I remember hearing how a farmer cried out that he did not even know how to hold a pen to make his mark on his passport. But he could balance two hundred pounds of rice on his right shoulder and walk five miles without taking a rest!

Kung shih fang literally means "public affairs room." Members of the kung shih fang paid very little "rent" (or membership dues), about $1 or $2 a month, and this was generally waived for people over sixty. The club rooms were a convenient way for the unemployed to seek work. They would show up offering their labor during the week, and by the weekend they had often found jobs in a laundry or restaurant. The kung shih fang was also a place for restaurant workers on the night shift to relax during the day.

Laundry work was considered better business than restaurant work because it took only four or five years to save enough money for a trip home to visit family. It was easy to save money, especially if one owned the business, because one could sleep there as well. Laundries were easy to sell, too, since buyers didn't have to spend much money for the takeover and there was little paperwork involved. This was especially true before 1934, because there were no license requirements for operating a laundry. In addition, laundry men saved on their own clothing expenses by appropriating customers' unclaimed shirts and pants!

In Chinatown, between Bayard and Canal Streets, there stands a huge building on Mott Street. It is called the Chinese Consolidated Benevolent Association (CCBA) and is considered the official spokesman and government of the Chinatown community. American and Chinese people alike call it the "Chinese City Hall." It represents more than seventy organizations, although some, such as On Leung Tong and Hip Sing Tong, for obvious reasons exert more power and control. The CCBA dates back to 1883, when it was registered with the Peking Imperial Government; now it is incorporated under New York law. A very tightly controlled group, it employs only four people—a chairman, English secretary, Chinese secretary, and custodian.

Before the turn of the century, the chairman usually did not need to know English. This exemption was customarily extended to those who had passed the Manchurian official examination in the capital of their province back home. The salary was not high, but chairmen, who served two-year terms, got lucrative commissions from the transactions of laundry and restaurant sales that took place within the organization. With organized gambling and the consequent corruption of the 1930s, however, a growing distrust grew up around this little "City Hall." When restaurants changed hands, owners began turning to lawyers instead of to the CCBA, and laundries simply put advertisements in the Chinese newspapers announcing the date and time (usually Monday at 12:00 noon) and conducted their transactions in the stores. Since the date and time were published, some gangs took advantage of the situation. One store was robbed of more than $10,000 and others of lesser but still large amounts, sometimes in the thousands. As a result, businesses began varying the times of these financial transactions.

When the CCBA caught on that it was no longer being used as middleman for the sales, it drastically cut its services to the community. People in the laundry business felt the repercussions for ten years. Before World War II there were about four thousand hand laundries in New York City; after the war the figure was reduced by almost one-half because shirt-pressing companies and big bosses of the wet-wash business had joined hands to monopolize the business. First they signed an agreement that wet-wash companies (to which individual laundry men farmed out much of their business), would not take away each other's customers. Then they raised the prices of wet-wash so unreasonably high that the hand laundry man could hardly make a profit. If anyone dared to raise his voice in protest, that wet-wash man just threw the key back to him and told him to find another wet-wash company, and the laundry man had to close his shop. The Caucasian wet-wash companies did the same thing.

The case was brought before the CCBA, but they never did a damn thing in defense of the poor laundry man. The laundry man had to raise his price per shirt so high that with the coming of "wash and wear" and "permanent press" fabrics he slowly became a legend of the past. People seemed to blame it on prices, but that was only part of it. I think it had more to do with the spirit of service. And so, years down the line, when I was able to establish my own business again, I turned not to the CCBA but to the Chinese Hand Laundry Alliance.

# The Cheating Game

As in any business, when one buys a hand laundry sometimes one meets a good man who is sincere in selling. Then there are also the not so good who just want to get rid of their laundries, well knowing there is no business at all. I was a victim of the latter type, of three Ma brothers notorious for opening new laundries and then selling them quickly for profit by exaggerating the amount of weekly business.

Kiu King, a member of the Lai clan and a friend of the Ma brothers, came and spoke with my elder cousin, the only one who had time to help me look for a hand laundry. He said that there was a laundry for sale in Harlem, with business amounting to $70 a week. The rent was $30 a month, and the laundry loads consisted of plenty of underwear, socks, handkerchiefs, and not too many shirts (shirts had to be sent out to shirt-pressing companies, which ate away profits). One could clear $40 a week, he said. This laundry was priced at $750, and I was desperate to have it. "Kiu King is one of those bad eggs who is known throughout the Lai clan," one of the old cousins, Yuen Suey, advised me. "The Ma's laundry might not have $70 worth of business weekly."

"Cousin Ming Wai told me the same story," I answered, "but I have no choice. In the first place, when I was in Boston, he promised to lend me $1,000; the week I came to New York he reduced that amount to $750. After another month, he said that all he could afford to lend me is $500.

For this reason I have to make the deal quickly before he changes his mind a third time."

I decided to take the risk and I was indeed cheated. The business amounted to only $30 a week. I couldn't even clear $10 out of that.

Kiu King was not without his sense of humor though. About two months after the sale he came to my laundry, but not to apologize. As soon as he sat down he asked, "Hey, did Ma's wife come here often?"

"Yes. She came here once a week, asking for the use of the toilet," I answered.

"You know what she means?"

"No. What does she mean?"

"Her husband sends her here purposely so you can take her to bed."

"Why?"

"She gave birth to three daughters but no sons, so her husband wants her to make a pass at you. He knows about your two sons back home."

"Nonsense! They cheated me on this laundry and now they want me to give them a son? Not bad!"

"Well, you can have a good time for nothing," he laughed.

"Of course, but I am not the type of man to do that." King related the conversation to Ma, and his wife never came around again.

# Turning to Wisdom

I had only three years of a high school education, but having a strong background in the Confucian classics and classical poetry, I felt that I was more prepared philosophically than the average Chinese immigrant to take up the challenges of life in Gold Mountain. Still, when I bought my laundry and had to confer with the landlord, I needed an interpreter. We laundry men had no knowledge of English, so we could not enjoy American movies either. Since there were no Chinese movies in the 1930s, the only amusement for us was the playing of mahjong or fan-tan.

After leaving the laundry one weekend and playing from midnight on Saturday until five o'clock the next Monday morning, I wandered home aimlessly, adjusting the collar of my heavy coat to ward against the March winds of a blustery cold 1937. As I shivered, I recalled a poem written by a poor gambler's wife:

> One can hardly ward against the cold with tattered clothes,
> Oh, my good man, come not home at five in the morn';
> Under a piercing wind and bitter moon, in the home,
> There awaits a four-year-old son in bed.[1]

Emperor Ch'ien Lung of the Ch'ing Dynasty amputated the gambler's ten fingers when he learned that the gambler's wife had hanged herself!

I was chilled to the bone. Reconsidering my life, I was determined to turn over a new leaf. I stopped gambling alto-

[1] Anonymous, Ch'ing Dynasty (1644–1911).

gether and used my spare time to study English—from nine o'clock at night until two in the morning, daily. In the winter of 1937 my laundry was very cold. It was located in a basement, and I smoked to keep warm. After I started to learn English, I immediately asked the director of the Chinese Hand Laundry Alliance to help write three letters for me, addressed respectively to St. John's, Fordham, and New York University, inquiring whether a high school dropout could ever hope to attend college. The only personal reply I received was from Dr. Ralph E. Pickett, then assistant dean of the School of Education at New York University. An immediate bond was established, one that would last a lifetime, as Dr. Pickett was most encouraging. He provided me with basic grammar books and continued sending literature throughout my years of service in the United States Navy.

I was reminded of a tale told to me in childhood: Once upon a time, an old man on the Chinese frontier lost his horse. When neighbors consoled him, he said, "Oh, couldn't this also be a blessing?" No sooner had the horse run away than he returned, bringing with him a stallion. The neighbors congratulated him, to which the old man said, "Couldn't this also be a misfortune?" After a while the son of the old man fell from the stallion and broke his arm. His neighbors came to offer condolences again, but the old man comforted himself saying, "Couldn't this all be providence?" Finally, his son was exempted from military service on account of the broken arm!

I had been cheated in the buying of the laundry, but it provided me with plenty of time to learn and study English. I considered myself as fortunate as the frontiersman who lost his horse and was blessed by providence. Setting down both Chinese and English versions of the Confucian classics side by side, I analyzed each phrase, word for word. When

I knew every word thoroughly, I repeated the same procedure with Chinese and English versions of the Bible. By
1939, I was the Sunday sermon interpreter at the True Light
Lutheran Church in New York's Chinatown!

# Gold Mountain Dreams

# A Navy Man

By 1941 I had already paid off half my debt and was hoping to go to college in a few years' time, but my dreams were shattered. On December 8, just one day after the infamous sneak attack on Pearl Harbor, the United States declared war on Japan. I joined the United States Navy three weeks later, on December 27, 1941, and took a loss on the laundry for which I had paid $750.

The entire world was fast becoming a war zone. Fighting had been going on in Europe since 1939 with the German invasion and occupation of Poland that September. This was followed in November by the Soviet attack on Finland, which was met by strong resistance from a defiant Finnish military. While the Russo-Finnish War ended by March 1940, the Germans continued to advance into Western Europe to conquer Norway and Denmark and to begin rounding up the Jews, a people singled out by Adolf Hitler during his 1933 election campaign for chancellor as being the cause of Germany's economic woes. By May 1940 German forces had advanced into Belgium and Holland. Both countries immediately appealed to London for help, and both Britain and France at once responded, although their forces were no match for German tanks and air power.

Neville Chamberlain resigned as prime minister on May 10 and was replaced by Winston Churchill. On Churchill's first day in office, British forces occupied the Danish dependency of Iceland, a strategic base that must not fall into the hands of the Germans, now that they were the rulers of

Denmark. The allies needed to develop Iceland's naval and air bases as quickly as possible. It was this aspect of the war that I watched with keen interest. The Arctic seas came to be an essential communications route, especially between British, North American, and North Russian ports, for the transfer of war supplies to the Soviet Union. Arctic territories provided approach routes or land bridges to strategically significant regions below the Arctic circle and also gave early warnings of meteorological conditions affecting sea and air operations in the lower latitudes. With Allied control over the Arctic region, German attempts to establish weather stations west of Norway were foiled.

Back home, even though President Franklin D. Roosevelt had vowed during his re-election campaign that the United States would remain neutral in any foreign wars, steps were being taken to support Great Britain in other ways. As Hitler and his commanders finalized their plans for the invasion of Russia in June 1941, Roosevelt froze all German and Italian assets in the United States. He also accepted Churchill's request for the United States to take over the defense of Iceland, and significant American arms and tanks were sent to British forces in Egypt in merchant ships flying the American flag. By July 1941, the United States had launched Operation Indigo, the landing of a Marine brigade in Iceland. Still, the burden of convoying ships remained with British and Canadian forces.

The war at sea fascinated me as an outside observer. But as the war escalated and turned global, recruitment posters started to appear on every corner. I grew nervous. Indeed, it was with the bombing of Pearl Harbor and the subsequent U.S. declaration of war on Japan that I actually feared being drafted into the army. I did not want to be a fighter on land; on land, one goes it alone, and one soldier can be shot and killed without his buddy next to him so much as getting a scratch. So to avoid being drafted into the army I joined the navy. At least on board a ship, when one gets hit we all go down together.

I was the first Chinese person in New York City to enlist in the navy, and photos of my swearing-in appeared in the two major Chinese newspapers there. These newspapers had nationwide circulation so the photos made for good promotion, as the U.S. Navy wanted to use them to encourage minority enlistment.

The status the navy allowed minorities was not particularly prestigious; we served mainly as waiters for the captains and admirals. At that time the U.S. Navy would not allow any people of color, Asians included, into any other division than the Mess Attendants'. They later changed that classification to "Stewards' Mates."

After three months of training I was assigned with two other Chinese men to the *U.S.S. Ranger,* an aircraft carrier, with the duties of serving the flag officers and the admiral at their tables, three meals a day. Besides this the three of us, under the orders of a Filipino steward, had to stand watch. The Filipino admiral boy was exempt from this duty. When we were on stand-watch duty at night we had to sleep on the floor in the small pantry, which was about five by ten feet, simply to make fresh coffee upon the ring of the telephone and to bring it up to the flag officers on watch duty up in the tower on the fly-deck when the ship was under way. On duty twenty-four hours a day, with a rotation every eight hours, the three of us could hardly get enough sleep during our time on sea duty.

Our destination was Iceland, the heart of the action for submarine warfare. With the development of British air bases in Iceland, German U-boats were gradually forced west of the North Atlantic. There was a severe shortage of aircraft, and the Americans' use of these Icelandic bases greatly increased the area of the North Atlantic that could be covered by air patrols. On April 1, 1942, I got my first taste of the war that I had followed with such enthusiasm as a civilian. Nineteen merchant ships, Convoy PQ 13, set sail from Iceland with war supplies for Russia. Five were sunk, and the principal escort, the cruiser Trinidad, was disabled by German torpedoes. On that same day, we heard, Operation Performance attempted to dispatch ten Norwegian merchant ships from Sweden to Great Britain; five were sunk by the Germans, another severely damaged, and two turned back; only two made it to Britain safely. A month and a half later, on May 14, German torpedo bombers sank the Trinidad as it escorted Allied merchant ships on the route of the Russian convoy run from Iceland to Archangel in the Soviet Union.

By January 1943 the United States and Great Britain had agreed at the Casablanca conference that their priority was to win the battle of the Atlantic. Additional long-range aircraft were allocated, and by March 1943 there was a marked increase in U-boat losses. That same month Allied powers deployed eighteen VLR (very long-range) patrol aircraft; and by May 1943 another forty-nine. Allied air power was becoming increasingly effective, as we could at once both harry U-boats gathered around convoys and attack in mid-ocean those U-boats that had to run on the surface in order to recharge their batteries. The defeat of the U-boats was confidently achieved by May 1943, with German navy and marine forces significantly reduced. They retained only a minor degree of effectiveness until the end of the war.

Through it all I marveled at how warplanes were
off and land on a narrow air strip. Like a child, I
planes disappearing into the mist and cheered ea
returned. I developed a true sense of power and national
pride for the first time in my life that made me realize how
far I had come from my humble roots in Sha-tou village.
From a weak China to an all-powerful United States Navy, I
was indeed proud that I had made it to Gold Mountain.

But this was the war. This was the *U.S.S. Ranger* I was on
board, not the real Gold Mountain to which I would have
to return when it was all over, where I would again have to
struggle to make my living. With the lack of sleep during sea
duty, I kept myself awake much of the time by rethinking
my situation in Gold Mountain. As a paper son, I had
entered the United States a "single" man. In reality I had a
wife and two sons back home to support, in addition to my
mother. Now, on a ship such as this aircraft carrier, the
admiral had his enemy to consider, as well as the men in his
task forces in the air and on the seas. The captain had his
administrative duties over the three thousand sailors in his
care. And I, a man of insignificant status, had my own trou-
bles as to how to keep my mother, wife, and two sons alive
on the mainland with only one abandoned house to live in
and no rice field to work at for their daily bread.

As soon as I was on board the *U.S.S. Ranger*, I made a $17
monthly allotment to my mother out of my monthly wage
of $34. All other papers were legally in the name of my
"paper" mother, but in the care of my most respected distant cousin who also happened to be a paper son. So it was
too with my $10,000 national life insurance policy provided
by the navy. By leaving my papers in the care of my cousin,
I made sure my paper mother would not get a windfall if I
got killed in action.

After I had made my allotment to my mother, Uncle Sam made a law providing for family subsidies. All the servicemen got a portion for their family allotment, $15 to each member of the family. I cursed my fate because I was registered as a single man when I came to the United States. In my mind I blamed my father for his shortsightedness in so arranging for my passage here. In this matter I lost thousands of dollars for my wife and two sons. But at least I could still apply for the government allotment for my mother, put in the care of my distant cousin.

When I did so, however, the officer in charge would not approve it at first, saying that government money could not be entrusted to a "friend."

"But before there was a law for the government allotment," I said, "I had already made my own allotment in care of my cousin. I trusted my own money to my cousin and now you mean to tell me that the government can't trust him for the few dollars?" The officer thought for a while and approved it. By so doing he inadvertently performed a very noble deed and saved four lives. For this matter came up in conversation later with other Chinese sailors at the naval base and those from the army camp. They were surprised to learn that I could arrange for the allotment to be paid that way; they tried to but could not do it. After I was discharged from the navy in 1945, the cousins of the clan told me that none of the Chinese servicemen in the New York area could arrange for it either. Their government allotments were all held in the Bank of China while their families literally died of starvation!

Well, as I see it, the law is flexible. The matter is entirely contingent upon the individual and how he handles his situation. My situation in particular was fairly simple—but then again, not all that simple; all did not work out in my favor. Just before my discharge the insurance officer asked me if I wanted to keep the $10,000 life insurance policy. Since the policy was in my paper mother's name alone I told him no. He replied, "You're a damn fool." He was absolutely right, but how was he to know the secrets of the Chinese paper son? I had to swallow my bitterness in silence.

Throughout my years of service in the navy, and through all of my personal concerns back home, I never lost sight of the possibility of someday pursuing a high school equivalency course and attending college from there. Dean Pickett was undoubtedly the most influential person in my life at that time, reminding me that my dreams were not to be abandoned and remaining my mentor throughout the war. In a lengthy letter dated March 8, 1944, he wrote:

Dear Tung Pok:

Many thanks for your letter of February 1, and for the package which came [one month] later, to be exact on March 2. You quite overwhelmed me, particularly since I just learned this week-end that there has been a further delay in shipping the subscription of the *Reader's Digest* to you together with the further difficulty in trying to acquire that high school education book about which I had written earlier. The subscription department of *Reader's Digest* has assured us that the first copies will eventually get to you, but we haven't been able to find out definitely whether it is a question of shortage of paper or whether it was a clerical error in their office or whether they are not allowed to take on a new subscriber until an old one drops out of the ranks, etc., etc. As for the book, it seems that a new edition is supposed to be coming on the market, although in the meantime none of the older editions are apparently available even in secondhand bookstores. I could not get a promise as to the date of publication of the new edition nor even any assurance that a new edition definitely would be produced. However, I shall keep on trying since although one cannot include within the covers of one book all that normally would be included in a four year high school education, nevertheless the material therein included should be more or less ideal for your purposes. This would be especially true if after your return from the service you were to make application for a comprehensive examination to cover part or all of the knowledge usually covered in four years of high school. There are such placement and competency examinations given in a number of institutions and you should certainly undertake to have yourself placed and classified at the first opportunity. The volume in question should help considerably in this effort. . . .

You have undoubtedly got a good deal of the right sort of stuff in you as evidenced by the marvelous improvement which you have made in your command of the English language. Your handwriting is immeasurably improved and, indeed, it is now a superior handwriting to that possessed by me or by my own children, for example, who have enjoyed the benefits of the best of our American schools. Your vocabulary is improving all the time and, indeed, were it not for the occasional lapses in the use of our idioms, it would be hard to detect that you had not learned to use our language in our traditional public schools. All of this is good evidence that you should be able to place reasonably well in any of the standard comprehensive examinations and if you retain your drive and your present interest in acquiring a formal education it should be possible to work out a plan to accomplish that end. . . .

No one can tell when this war will be over or how soon you as an individual will return to these shores and, hence, no one can guess what conditions will face us when you actually do return. However, if the situation in my household is the same at that time as it is now, Mrs. Pickett and I would very much like to have you take dinner with us some time when we can fit it into our respective calendars. I know that we and our youngsters would enjoy hearing of your experiences and we, in turn, might perhaps be able to bring you up-to-date on some aspects of life as it has been lived in this country during your absence. Best of luck to you.

Cordially yours,
Ralph E. Pickett

# A New Outlook

The war did finally end, and I returned to New York. Penniless, I sought work as a laundry helper at various shops until I could save enough money to purchase my own business again. When I was ready to set out on my own, I joined the Chinese Hand Laundry Alliance (CHLA), which helped me obtain the proper papers. The alliance also organized to protect the rights of laundry workers, settling any customer or legal disputes. In those days, anyone could seek counsel from the CHLA for only twenty-five cents. We were like family, especially since we all spoke the Tai-shan dialect from back home. Sometimes when I was lonely, I would go there just for fellowship.

I also resumed my post as interpreter at the True Light Lutheran Church on Sundays. While this was a volunteer post, it was also a social event that diverted me from the routine chores of the laundry and provided me the opportunity to put my English to good use. I was already somewhat of a celebrity in New York's Chinatown, due mainly to my photo promotion for the U.S. Navy, but with this added duty I now had the confidence of the community as well. Standing beside the pastor of the church each week earned me the honorary nickname "Pastor Lai."

In my spare time I took up writing. I had plenty of experiences to write about since traveling with the Navy allowed me to see many places and experience many things that I would never have been able to do on my own. My entire outlook on the world had changed; I saw everything through different eyes, and I became more involved in politics and world affairs.

When it came time to find a publisher for my works, I instinctively chose the *China Daily News*. It was, in my opinion, the more open-minded of the two Chinese newspapers in print at that time, and I wanted the truth about what was going on. For although the war in Europe was over, a bloody civil war had erupted in China between a strong Communist movement and a steadily weakening and corrupt Nationalist front backed by the United States. The *China Daily News* reported news of the battle directly from the Chinese mainland, whereas the other newspaper carried a Nationalist bias and refused to report accurately the events of a losing Nationalist front. The *China Daily News* was established in 1940 by the CHLA and supported by the capital of laundry workers, its main focus then being to keep the Chinese community informed of war efforts against Japan. Afterward it continued to bring news directly from the mainland.

Naturally the Chinese community rallied behind the United States, since it was China's ally. The issue then was not Nationalist vs. Communist but the wish to see a defeated Japan and a strong China. Many times, I felt secretly ashamed of my homeland. People looked down on the Chinese, I sensed, because China was so weak. Back home, I couldn't make a living; abroad, I was mocked. Even little children called out derogatory names to me as they passed by my laundry, or as I sometimes walked through the neighborhood streets. If China were strong, I thought, then our image here would also be strong; if China were strong, many of us would not have had to go overseas to begin with.

So at the CHLA we did what we could to help China. We collected money to buy ambulances and to help with medical and other relief efforts in the war against Japan. As long as the United States and China were allies, that worked out. But after the war, things changed. In 1949 Communist forces took control of the mainland. A year later, they fought against the United States in the Korean War. Overnight the CHLA and the *China Daily News* were charged with engaging in pro-Communist activities. While Nationalist supporters organized a boycott of the newspaper, its subscribers were instantly accused of being Communist sympathizers. I, unfortunately, fell into this category. Still, I was anxious to be a published poet and took my chances.

At the *China Daily News* I was introduced to Mr. T'ang Ming Chao, then editor of the paper. He was tall compared with the average Chinese person, with a medium build and wire-framed glasses. His shoes were worn to the soles, and his pants were mended in the seat with a patch as large as the full moon! Appearances aside, one immediately sensed his acute intelligence and natural leadership abilities. He was discussing classical literature with a colleague and expressed specifically a desire to learn to compose poetry. Since I had studied classical poetry in depth both in school and on my own, we quickly became friends, and I became his tutor. Our relationship never extended beyond the workplace, but we did often share the same table at supper time.

I became more involved with writing, prolifically churning out poems on Gold Mountain, my home village in China, war, peace, life, and death, and they were all published—hundreds of them over the course of the next few years! I was excited by my newfound talent and minor success. I no longer dreamed of going to college. In my heart, I had always felt that it was a bit unrealistic anyway. Now, I wanted to make a name for myself as a poet. And I knew that if I could succeed anywhere in the world, it would be in Gold Mountain—the land of opportunity!

# The "Confession Period"

It is commonly said among us Chinese here in the United States that before World War II about 99 percent of all Chinese immigrants were paper sons. For this reason most Chinese GIs were not permitted to bring their families, brothers, or sisters, to settle here. If they wished to do so, they first had to make confession before the immigration officials so as to change their status. By confessing their true names, ages, and personal data, they would live legitimately as permanent residents, with eligibility for naturalization after the then required five-year residency period.

I never made confession the way so many others did. I was born in China during a time of intense internal turmoil. The Manchu Government, or Ch'ing Dynasty, had just collapsed and been replaced by the new "Republic," and warlords still roamed the village countryside, supporting themselves by stealing, robbing, and kidnapping young babes and toddlers to sell to wealthier, barren couples. This, unfortunately, was what had happened to me.

Kidnapped and sold to the Lai family, I never knew my true name, much less my date or place of birth; therefore, I never confessed. My name as a paper son was Chin Tung Pok. The family that purchased me as a boy of three named me Lai Bing Chan. Since I entered the United States as Chin Tung Pok, I adopted Lai Bing Chan as my pen name when I started to write. Being a man of principle, confession merely meant replacing one false name with another, so there was no point in it for me. But I did not know that by

52

not confessing I would run into serious problems in the McCarthy years to come. Confession, as it turned out, was a way for the government to distinguish between who was here legally and who was not.

During the so called "confession period," which lasted from shortly after World War II to 1970, innumerable stories were reported in the Chinese newspapers of how immigration officials and FBI agents tried to root out paper sons, asking questions at Chinese laundries and restaurants, searching stores and homes without a warrant. At a neighboring laundry on Central Avenue in Brooklyn, a certain Mr. Wong told me that immigration officials had come to his store and turned everything upside down. His son was of his own flesh and blood, but both came under the paper name "Lee." In time, it became clear that these unlawful searches were not so much due to legal concerns about false papers as to the fear of communism.

But it is only in retrospect that the pieces of this puzzle fit together. For in the years following the war, there were already major changes on the international political scene that caused the United States to cast a wary eye on communism at home and abroad. Many of the Eastern European nations had turned to communism, and strong communist parties existed in Italy and France, not to mention in the USSR, which had been lost to communism since 1917. Now Nationalist and Communist factions fought to gain control of the Chinese mainland. This civil war was followed intently by "China watchers" in the United States, and many had already predicted a Communist victory well before it occurred.

On October 1, 1949, the Nationalists surrendered the mainland to the Communists, fled to the island of Taiwan under

U.S. protection, and established their base there for the Republic of China. Meanwhile, the Communists celebrated their victory on the mainland and declared it the People's Republic of China.

Early in the following year, the Smith Act was applied in full force against all American communists in the United States, declaring it illegal for any person to become a member or affiliate of any group that advocated the violent overthrow of the U.S. government. The act directly contradicted the First Amendment and introduced for the first time in United States jurisprudence the concept of "guilt by association." Nevertheless, it was thought that the threat posed by communism at that time was so great that the constitutional guarantee of the First Amendment had to give way.

On February 9, 1950, Senator Joseph McCarthy, Republican of Wisconsin, announced that he had a list of over two hundred names known by the secretary of state to be members of the Communist Party, yet these people were still working and shaping policy in the State Department. Within the next two years he established his own investigative teams to search for communists in every walk of life. Thousands of American citizens were dismissed from their places of employment or denied employment for mere association with a political way of thinking, and literally millions of others lived in strictest conformity for fear that the same might happen to them.

Paranoia swept the nation, and the effects of this on the Chinese communities throughout the United States were devastating. While many Chinese professionals and workers quickly adopted apolitical views, others who had been apolitical quickly adopted pro-Nationalist positions for fear of appearing disloyal before U.S. authorities and thus risking deportation. Most letter writing between relatives on the mainland ceased, and those who continued to write suspected their mail had been opened; other cases of mail tampering were quite obvious. Bookstores and newspaper stands refused to carry literature from "Red" China for fear of being cast as sympathizers with the Communist cause; and Chinese storekeepers had to unload their inventory of Chinese products lest they too be accused of being supporters. In short, all ties to the mainland had to be severed.

Yet, despite a news blackout, new immigrants from Guangdong Province via Hong Kong inevitably brought news, memories, and experiences with them. The *China Daily News* was the only remaining newspaper in New York's Chinatown that would accept and print their stories. It was, in my opinion, the most objective newspaper in the Chinese community. It was for this reason that I subscribed to the paper and chose it as the instrument of publication for my poetry.

Now, the editor of the *China Daily News,* Mr. T'ang Ming Chao, was an avowed Communist who returned to the Chinese mainland soon after the Communist victory. I heard nothing further of him until twenty-five years later, when I read of his return to the United States as a member of the first Chinese delegation to the United Nations. His daughter, Brooklyn-born Nancy T'ang, would become well known to the West as an interpreter for President Richard M. Nixon on his visit to China in 1972.

It was soon after Mr. T'ang's departure for China that all those who remained loyal subscribers and contributors to the *China Daily News* were automatically suspected of communist involvement. The worst accusation came in 1950, when the newspaper accepted advertisements from Chinese banks encouraging Chinese Americans to send money to relatives in China through it. We already sent money as individuals to help support our families, but because of the ads the *China Daily News* was charged with violating the Trading with the Enemy Act and the Foreign Assets Control Regulations by engaging in a conspiracy to induce Chinese people in America to send remittances to China to further the aims of the Chinese Communist government. Eugene Moy, who succeeded Mr. T'ang as editor of the *China Daily News,* was sent to jail.

# A Bitter End, a Bright Sta

Meanwhile, back home, my mother and my two sons settled in Hong Kong, but my wife did not; she delayed joining the family until several months later. She was unfaithful; she had an affair with the son of my mother's sister, gave birth to a baby girl, and buried it in a heap of ashes.

I had suspected that something was wrong because soon after I was discharged from the navy my mother brought her sister's eldest son to Hong Kong to stay in the house; it was shortly afterward that my wife rejoined the family. I wrote to my mother asking her not to keep him there, but she chided me for being unfilial and disrespectful toward her wishes. She said he had become unwell during the war and needed care. After reading her letter I wondered why I should be so much against the will of a woman who brought me up as her own son—simply for the preservation of another woman, my wife. My mother was fifty-nine; her nephew was thirty; my wife was thirty-four. That was 1945. They had an affair, in which my mother was complicit, and the young man died in this lewdness soon after the war's end.

I surrendered. By registered mail I returned the wedding ring to my wife and ordered her to leave the house. My mother kept supporting her all the years from 1945 to 1951. She spent my money carelessly, spending many times more than was necessary for a family of that size. I had hoped that she would plan better for the future so that I could one day retire and live comfortably in Hong Kong, but my dreams for a happy family reunion were now gone.

The two sons of this ill-fated marriage, Lai Wai Sing and Lai Wai Yong, were very intelligent. The school they attended was the best in Hong Kong—Pui Ching Middle School, operated by the Baptist Church. For years they remained at the top of the honor rolls. Encouraged by their diligence, I had no plans to remarry, intending to give them the best education possible with all my earnings in the years to come.

One day in 1948 Sing Suey told me that his wife was coming to the United States on board the *U.S.S. Gordon,* bringing in all the Chinese GI families in one load, and that there was room to bring in two more paper sons. He asked if I wanted to take advantage of this. It would be easy, he said, no questions asked, not even by Immigration. I told him, "No. I will not bring my sons into the United States to be waiters or laundry men. If they come, they will eventually come as students."

Apparently, without my prior approval or knowledge, my sons had already been approached about the possibility of coming to Gold Mountain. Perhaps they idealistically pictured Gold Mountain as a place where streets are paved with gold; whatever the temptation, they wanted desperately to come and lost heart when I would not bring them here. Their grades dropped. I rushed to Hong Kong early in 1949 in an attempt to salvage their academic futures. I tutored the older son, Wai Sing, in English and the younger, Wai Yong, in mathematics. They managed to pass on reexamination, but when I returned to the United States that spring they failed again—and again.

Seeing that my sons had not the slightest inclination toward study, I decided to marry a second time. My first marriage was not legal in the eyes of United States jurisprudence, since I was reported as single when I went through the Immigration House. That spared me the time and expense of a formal dissolution of it. Now, with a fresh start, I could not object to my lot in life, save what heaven had predestined for me.

In the summer of 1949, I returned to Hong Kong again, a "Gold Mountain" man with a specific goal in mind. I was an honorably discharged U.S. naval man and I had saved up enough money to purchase my own laundry business and finally be my own boss again. Thus, I was a "good catch."

Sing Suey, my cousin by paper, was the matchmaker. My new bride would be his wife's sister. This meant that we would no longer be just "paper cousins" but real in-laws.

My new wife, Mak Ting Fong, came from a prominent family in Hong Kong. Her father, an Oxford graduate, was an English teacher; her mother, a midwife who herself bore nine children (two of whom died during the war), was able to retire at the ripe young age of forty-five. They had been settled in Hong Kong for six generations already. Saddened by a bomb-ravaged homeland, they were now eager to see as many of the next generation off to America as possible.

While I was eager to start a new family, there were also deep reservations within me. What right had I to offer my hand in marriage to a young woman and to bring her to Gold Mountain to live the life of a laundry man's wife, when I refused to bring even my own sons here to live? Thus, I counseled her that laundry work is hard, the days are long and strenuous, and the streets are not paved with gold. The final decision would rest with her.

That summer we were married in a modest ceremony in Hong Kong. She bore our first child, a boy, as we crossed the Pacific Ocean aboard the *U.S.S. Wilson* in the spring of 1950. We named him Wilson, after the ship that brought us to

America! In 1952, she gave birth to a daughter, Winifred. After three sons, I was so happy to see a baby girl that my eyes swelled with tears at the sight of her! It was to me a sign that things would be different from now on.

Late that same year, the distant cousin to whom I had entrusted my monthly allotment while I was in the navy came to my laundry. He asked me to give my mother a lump sum of $2,000, in the care of his wife, so that she could marry off Wai Sing and care for herself in her old age. This request I honored, taking advantage of the opportunity to grant her a final wish and cut off ties with her completely. Having foreseen World War II as inevitable, I had bought a $2,000 fifteen-year endowment policy from the U.S. Life Insurance Company. I surrendered it before its maturity to fulfill my commitment. I was now poor as a dog. Since then I have never written to her again. She raised me, built me a family, and then ruined it with her own irresponsibility and complicity in my first wife's affair. It was a tragic disaster. I had no more tears to shed, no, not even a drop when I heard of her death later that year.

Soon afterward, I wrote to my former wife to offer condolences. Her reply, written in her own pen, confessed the truth that I had hoped would someday be manifest:

Dear Husband:

Thank you for your letter. I am mixed in thoughts as I read it. . . . I was young, sleeping alone; I felt cold under the comforter and on the pillow, but was willing to be a Gold Mountain wife. I had no complaints. I was dreaming that one day you would return home with plenty of money, and we would spend the rest of our lives happily together . . . but then mother-in-law took [him] into the house and I fell into their trap. . . . It was my mistake, but mother-in-law was not without fault. . . . After V-Day you asked me to leave the house, and I knew I had no right to beg for your pardon. I did as you asked. . . .

When you returned to Hong Kong in '49 you didn't even pay me a visit in my mother's house, but now you want your sons to marry and bring me home to enjoy the life that a mother-in-law should have. . . . Are you now feeling sorrow for me? I know my life was unfortunate and I am unworthy of your blessing.

I hear there is another one in your life now. She is more deserving of this happiness as mother-in-law. I shall be satisfied if you allow the two sons to visit me every now and then. As for myself, my broken heart has found one who accepts me. You shall not worry for me from now on; but your two sons, they are your flesh and blood. My wrong has nothing to do with them; don't let them suffer. Wishing you luck with your new wife. . . .

Yours truly . . .

# A Paper Son's Duty

One day in the spring of 1952, shortly before our daughter was born, my wife received a telephone call that brought at once both pleasantly surprising and startling news. Her youngest brother, whom we called "B7" (seventh baby of the family), barely fifteen years of age, had arrived in New York from Hong Kong. She could hardly believe it! He had actually arrived several months before, but he was advised by his "paper" family not to contact us until things were more settled, since he, too, had come as a paper son.

One evening, however, B7 managed to slip away. He came to our laundry and cried his heart out, just like the baby that he indeed was.

"When did you arrive here?" I asked.

"Three months ago. The family wouldn't tell me where you were. They said it would threaten their status if the authorities discovered I was really related to you instead."

"Where are you staying?"

"In New Jersey. They have a small laundry at Union Turnpike. I slept on an army cot. One night I overheard Uncle Hom telling his wife that they were losing money keeping me there, so they sent me to Paterson to learn to be a waiter."

My wife was speechless as B7 continued his story. He had come to the United States as the "nephew" of Hom Suey Wah. Now, Hom Suey Wah was from the back country of Tai-shan, China. A struggling farmer, he spoke a country dialect unknown to most Hong Kong natives, B7 included. Hom Suey Wah also had six paper brothers. All this worked against B7, because the more brothers and sisters you have, the more factual data you have to memorize for questioning. Along with his mother, B7 practiced day in and day out, trying to sound and act like Tai-shan country folk. He even dressed accordingly, just like a country farmer, and insisted that his mother do the same at the U.S. General Consulate in Hong Kong. They were not convincing, though. The paper broke in Hong Kong. He begged his mother for support and came here anyway to appeal. When this innocent fifteen-year-old arrived and found that there was no gold to be got from the streets of Gold Mountain, he wanted desperately to return to Hong Kong.

As I saw it, though, the real victim would be Hom Suey Wah, B7's "paper" uncle, if B7 actually confessed and returned home. I tried to reason with him to do what was proper.

"In the first place," I told him firmly, "your 'Uncle Hom' already told your 'aunt' in Hong Kong not to accept you. How will you return home if your 'relative' denies you sponsorship? It will leave you no choice but to confess your proper status and be your own free man again. That leads us to the second choice. In a confession you will totally destroy not only Hom Suey Wah's livelihood by exposing his paper status, but you will destroy the lives of your other 'uncles' as well. Remember, Uncle Hom has six paper brothers. They have done you absolutely no wrong. We all warned you that life in Gold Mountain is very hard, but you wouldn't listen to any of us. Now you want to return home. Well, you can't just leave. You've decided that you don't like the United States, but to people like Hom Suey Wah, to those from the poor villages of Tai-shan, the United States is paradise! They are not breaking their backs plowing a plot of land from dawn to dusk for the rest of their lives; they have shoes to wear when they work; they have good food to eat; and they have money to spend. This is glory for them! Your fourth 'uncle' came with me on the same boat at the age of thirty-five. The paper cost him $3,500. I met him on the street the other day. He told me he has never gone back home, not even for a visit. He's been here eighteen years now. This is their life, and you mustn't destroy it now. Gold Mountain may not be what you imagined it to be, but for others the myth is very real."

B7 listened intently, nodding at my words. He knew the proper thing to do. After a long pause, he said in a lowered voice, "Well, Gold Mountain was just too good a name to hear and not pursue. After all, one always believes only the good."

B7 refused to return to New Jersey that night. Instead, he took a room at the YMCA in Brooklyn while trying to figure a way out of his predicament. We, of course, had advised him against coming to the United States from the very start, clearly stating the limited options that most Chinese immigrants have here and encouraging him to continue with his studies in Hong Kong. His elder brother, who remained in Hong Kong, was already a senior at Hong Kong University Medical School and had promised to help finance B7's way through college as soon as he himself had graduated and set up private practice. B7, however, was sidetracked by stories of grandeur in Gold Mountain. After all, his eldest sister, Sing Suey's wife, had come here only a few years before us, and she was constantly sending money home. She and Sing Suey spoke often of early retirement and how they would save every penny they earned, exchange their U.S. funds for Hong Kong dollars, and return to Hong Kong in a style befitting millionaires! The shame is that most Chinese immigrants come to Gold Mountain with similar dreams of returning to the motherland in style. Few do, but those who fail to do so are too embarrassed or ashamed to relay the truth back home, and so the myth continues.

While he awaited the outcome of the appeal, B7 did go to Paterson to learn the ropes of the restaurant trade. From that spring night on, for the next ten months, his permanent home remained a rented room at the YMCA as he studied and apprenticed at various restaurants in New Jersey.

One night in the late winter of 1953, B7 came to my laundry disheartened. "The appeal is overthrown," he said. "They're sending me back to Hong Kong. I am in $1,000 bond if I jump bail and remain."

"Who bailed you out?" I asked.

"Uncle Hom managed to get together some money from his brothers and relatives. They were afraid that if they allowed the authorities to send me away it would be an admission of guilt and proof that we are not related. They don't want any trouble, so they put up the money to show that they're standing up for 'family.' Now they want me to stick to my story and remain in the United States."

Given B7's circumstances, the easy way out would have been to surrender to the authorities. He would then be returned to Hong Kong, just as he wished to be. But he confronted the situation, realizing the danger posed to his "paper" relatives if he admitted his true status and allowed himself to be deported. He was now determined to act for the common good, and so he jumped bail and ran—like an outlaw.

For the next two years, B7 went into hiding and worked "under the table," and for the lowest wages, at any restaurant in New York's Chinatown that would offer him work. It was pitiful. He was exploited to the fullest. In light of his situation, his paper family would have no more to do with him; and we, his closest kin here in Gold Mountain, were unable to acknowledge any relations at all because according to our papers we were not supposed to be related!

Whenever he got the chance B7 would come to visit us in Brooklyn, mostly at night so as not to be followed. He watched as my son and daughter, his true nephew and niece, frolicked and played during their growing years. Often, with his humble wages, he bought toys for the children and joined them at play. For he, too, deep down inside, was still a child of only sixteen! We were the only family he knew now. Still, my children never called him "uncle" as was his proper due. Because we were not related by paper, he was always the mysterious "B7" who came to visit with laughter, warmth, and toys. It was not until my children were mature enough to understand the secrets of the paper son that we sat down and explained everything to them.

Since B7 and my family had no relationship according to our papers, there was no reason for immigration officials to tail him to my laundry—yet they did. In the spring of 1954, when Winifred was barely two years old, two officers came to my store. After identifying themselves, one of them held up a picture of B7 as he carefully examined my wife's face from a distance of about ten feet.

"He's your brother, isn't he?" the officer asked my wife point-blank. "Your faces look exactly alike." Although my wife had a working knowledge of English, she was nervous and pretended not to understand.

"They're brother and sister all right," the other agreed.

"No, no. We are only friends," I said in a calm voice, hoping to dispel their suspicions.

"Why does he get his mail here?" the first one asked again.

"He uses this as a mailing address. He is in transit and has no home, and I give it to him whenever I see him in Chinatown."

"Has he ever lived here?" the agent persisted.

"No, never," I replied, shaking my head.

"Give me his address," the officer demanded. In order to get rid of them I gave them the address of the restaurant in New Jersey where B7 first apprenticed.

About an hour later I received a telephone call from the officer in New Jersey, saying, "He is not here. You told him to run, didn't you?"

"Yes," I admitted. There were no further questions, but I sensed from that moment on that before long I too would have to answer for events in my own life. As for B7, I had advised him when he turned eighteen to enlist in the U.S. Army. He did. That was the spring of 1955. Immigration tried to get him out, but he was on tour in Europe before they could track him down again. Entangled in their own governmental red tape, they failed at several future attempts, and by that time B7 was already safe under military supervision and law.

# Under Suspicion

It was the Spring of 1955. Winifred had just turned three and was a proud little girl at that. She had learned all of the vital information necessary for a three-year-old to be returned home in the event she wandered too far one day, and I had started her and Wilson on the first of the Chinese classics, the *Analects of Confucius*.

During the spring and summer months I usually left the front door of the laundry open because the heated irons and collar presser always made the place very hot. One day, I believe it was in May, when Wilson was still in school, two well-dressed men walked into my laundry. They introduced themselves as agents from the Federal Bureau of Investigation. Winifred, who had been playing on the front step, quickly turned around to see what was going on, as the two men had a very authoritative air about them. Now, in the laundry a wooden counter divided my general work area from the customer area, but because of a lack of space on my side of the counter the collar and cuff presser was placed in a corner on the customer side. I happened to be working on the collar presser on the customer side when the two men entered. Winifred, clutching her doll, came in after them and snuggled up behind me.

"Lai Bing Chan?" the taller man asked.

"Tung Pok Chin," I replied, sticking to the name and information on my paper. Just then, the other officer turned his attention to my daughter.

"What's your name, little girl?" he asked.

"Chin," my daughter answered quite matter-of-factly and with a firm nod of the head.

"You like candy?" the other one asked as he took a piece from the tin of sweets that I placed on the counter top for customers. Winifred did not come forward for it. "What's your daddy's name?" he continued.

"Chin," she answered again. He picked her up and sat her on the counter top, smiling as he did so. She did not respond with like friendliness, but stared outside longingly, her mind set on returning to play with her friends. They sent her back out to play. Now it was my turn.

"Mr. Chin, we have reason to believe that you are a Communist," asserted the taller agent in a straightforward tone of voice. His accusation came as no surprise, but in all fairness I felt that he at least could have used the word "suspect" rather than "believe."

"I am not a Communist. I belong to no party," I replied.

"But you support the Communist cause, do you admit?"

"No, you are wrong."

"You subscribe to the *China Daily News*. It is a pro-Communist paper."

"The *China Daily News* reports news from the mainland, so I read it," I explained.

"And you are interested in that part of the world?"

"I was born there, so I am interested in knowing about what is going on there. Besides, there is no other paper in Chinatown that reports on China now. They are all afraid; they don't want to be blacklisted. People don't want trouble; they don't want to risk being deported."

"You also write for the paper."

"I am only a subscriber," I said.

"Do you know Lai Bing Chan? You know, Chinatown is a very close-knit community. We have film footage of all those entering and leaving the *China Daily News* office and you are clearly identified by people citing both names. We've been watching you for quite some time now."

"I do not see the harm in anyone writing a few poems," I commented, all the while careful not to hint that I indeed was the writer.

"You know T'ang Ming Chao, former editor of the *China Daily*?"

"Yes. He is no longer living in the U.S."

"They say that you and he were very close friends. He was also an avowed Communist. To what extent was your relationship?"

"We were not close friends. When I first met him, I did not even know that he was a Communist. We never discussed politics. We talked about poetry and when he asked and discovered that I had studied the classics, he asked if I would teach him. I showed him some of my own works as well; he liked them and made the offer to publish some of them. That was all. He knew that I wanted to make a name for myself as a poet."

"You use the name Lai Bing Chan?"

"No."

"Was there any other relationship?" he pressed.

"No, that was all. He returned to the Chinese mainland after the Communist victory in 1949, and I have had no communications with him since." Indifferent as to what else they might ask, I returned to my work and the two officials seemed satisfied with my answers, at least for now. They were polite as they left, but their farewell indicated that they would be back again. They patted Winifred on the head as they walked past her.

Since coming to the United States, I had never used any name other than my name as a paper son, Tung Pok Chin, in any official, governmental way. The name Lai Bing Chan had never appeared on any personal papers or official documents, so there was absolutely no direct link between the two names. Lai Bing Chan could have been anyone's pseudonym. The only supporting evidence officials had was some film footage, with photos made from it, and people who identified me by two different names. You see, in the Chinese community we freely revealed ourselves and our past because we all knew how most of us got here. Often in conversation we would openly discuss our backgrounds, our villages, the people we knew, and address one another by our real names. We felt we were among family and we could be ourselves again, all sticking together in a foreign land. For official purposes we always resorted to the information on paper, but in reality no one could live a lie forever. How else would we know if a distant cousin had arrived? We only spoke the truth among ourselves. I suppose that was how the FBI made the connection between my two names: Simply ask a person in the Chinese community to identify me!

# A Dream in Flames

The first years of our home life were peaceful. We could almost have passed for the typical postwar nuclear family. I operated the laundry full-time to support my family, while Ting Fong remained at home with our two children. I worked hard six days a week, taking off only on Sunday when we went to Chinatown on family outings. There, each Sunday morning, I assumed my position once again as interpreter at the True Light Lutheran Church for the Reverend Louis T. Buchheimer. Church was also the center of our social life, the place where we met friends and where our children got to play with other children. My wife especially found escape there, after being alone with the children so much of the week. It was there that she eventually learned of the world of working women in the sweatshops of Chinatown. Such work was one of the few employment options for women with little or no knowledge of English. So it was that soon after Wilson started school in 1955, Ting Fong joined the Chinatown workforce. Our arrangement was convenient. The elementary school, Public School 116, was just three blocks from our storefront/residence. Ting Fong would leave Winifred with me in the laundry, take Wilson to school, and proceed to Chinatown from there. I would pick him up after school, supervise him while he did his homework, and sit both him and his sister down to study the Chinese classics. They were then allotted one hour of playtime before supper. Wilson was five and Winifred three.

I had studied the classics from the "old school," where one learned by rote, so while I ironed shirts and handkerchiefs, I simultaneously recited them line by line. My children followed in print, repeating after me, connecting the sounds, tones, and pronunciations of each character as they read on. This took about one-half hour. They then wrote out each phrase, first in pen, then in brush style Chinese calligraphy. I also taught them Chinese classical poetry, history, and geography. As a result, they were well occupied most afternoons and evenings. In the midst of McCarthyism, I felt that if ever it came to the point where we had to leave the country and return to China, it was important for our children to know about China and to know the language and culture there.

Ting Fong returned home every evening at about 9:00 P.M. Life as a seamstress in the sweatshops of Chinatown was harsh in those days. The hours were long, the conditions were poor, there were no benefits, and seamstresses were paid by the piece. Under the piecework system, the faster one worked, the greater the pay for both employee and employer. If one complained about conditions or took too long a lunch break, the employer simply fired the employee and hired someone else. Working too slowly was also a cause for termination, since a slow worker was seen as taking up valuable space and machinery that could be better used by someone more productive.

Although the International Ladies Garment Workers' Union (ILGWU) had been founded by 1900, the shops of Chinatown were uncharted territory, and organizers had only begun talking to workers and negotiating with shopkeepers in the early 1950s. Thus most sweatshops operated into the wee hours of the morning. Ting Fong often spoke of working until the close of shop like many of her coworkers, but I discouraged it. Working so late is bad enough when one lives within close proximity of the workplace, but to have to travel by subway for another hour to get home is self-punishment. Work, after all, was something she wanted just for herself as a means to get away from the house a bit. Since my income at the laundry was sufficient to support our modest lifestyle, anything she brought home would be her own to lavish on herself and the children. We also did not have to pay for child care, since I was home all day tending the laundry anyway. I was also able to prepare the meals between customers and laundry chores so that she could eat a hearty meal when she returned home.

At that hour there was usually not much talk at dinner. On the day the FBI agents came to the laundry, however, I told her about the visit. After the children were tucked into bed we discussed precautions we should take in case of a house search, not an uncommon event in those days.

That very night, we carefully wrapped all our back issues of Chinese newspapers with back issues of the *New York Times* and threw them away (we subscribed to the "pro-Nationalist" Chinese newspaper as well as to the *China Daily News*, but that did not seem to make any difference to officials). By not hanging onto the Chinese papers, we thought we would appear, in our own little way, more "American." The idea seems a bit silly now, but at the time it seemed the patriotic thing to do. The poetry that I wrote, more than two hundred poems published between 1945 and 1955, poems I had carefully cut out of each issue of the *China Daily News* and pasted into scrapbooks, were all taken out and burned. What reason would I, Tung Pok Chin, have for collecting the poetry of Lai Bing Chan, a writer for some "pro-Communist" paper?

I could not hold back the tears as I watched my life's work literally go up in flames. I once had visions of binding my poetry into a book for publication. Perhaps some Chinese American scholar would come across it and translate it into English, I thought. With such a detailed record of immigrant life, the old home town, the history and emotions of the paper son, I would really gain recognition as a poet! But now, all was lost.

Winifred woke up in the middle of the night to use the bathroom. She paused sleepy-eyed to look at the flames from the burning of my works and asked what we were doing.

"Just creating a little fire to warm our hands," I said. "But don't you try it," I gently warned her. She went to the bathroom and returned to bed. She did not ask about it again the next day, or ever, but when she was old enough to understand current events and to read about the McCarthy Era on her own, I reminded her of that night. She remembered it as a dream, she would later tell me . . . vague, but very real in its own way.

# Chinese Communism

I was never a communist, nor did I ever support the violent overthrow of the United States government. I have to admit that life in Gold Mountain has been good for me despite the long, hard hours of a laundry man's work, despite the language barrier at first, and despite McCarthyism in later years. However, my thoughts for China were altogether different, and not in accordance with those of mainstream American thought. I was born and raised in China, a country then overrun by warlords, and for most of my childhood, until I left my village, I knew nothing but hunger and deprivation. Such a life was typical.

My own theory is that communism works only in a country where the masses are abused and discontented to the point that they would join forces to overthrow the existing ruling order. As I saw it, this was the case in China, but not in the United States. That McCarthyism ever happened, or that communism was ever even thought to be a threat to the government here, was preposterous. I have had many a long discussion late into the night, and exchanged many letters, with my faithful friend Ralph Pickett about this. While we never quite reached a common understanding regarding which path was best for China, we did find some common ground of belief and hope. In a letter of September 1, 1950, he wrote:

> I can well understand the enthusiasm in some quarters of
> China and among some people for the change in regime. The
> New York Times is usually a reasonably faithful reporter, but

as I have read its columns year in and year out, I have noticed about as many stories on the one side as there have been on the other. I think this is entirely understandable. All one needs to do is to put himself in the place of one of those terribly abused, poor farmers. Almost any change would be for the better, at least temporarily.

Having been in the shoes of the "abused, poor farmer," I naturally felt the change in China to be for the better. Yet, as Dr. Pickett continued:

One can also put himself in the place of the landowner, who for centuries has felt that it is entirely right for him to carry on the way that he has been doing. Naturally, the confiscation of his land seems to him a gross injustice, and certainly if he is lined up and shot against the wall that makes, for him and his family, an even greater injustice in his own mind. In effect then, to the man who has nothing at all, a change whereby something is given to him, is in his eyes a fine thing, even though that which is given to him may have been confiscated from somebody else.

While it is true that one must consider the rights of the landowner too, it is also true that privileged Chinese land-owners accounted for only a small minority of the population, while underprivileged peasant farmers made up the majority of the starving masses. In my study of history I have never come across an upper class that voluntarily gave up its power in exchange for equality with the lower classes. For the rich and privileged to give up power, they must sense the force of the assembled masses opposing them. Only then do the moral ideals of the aristocracy give way to the demands of the long-neglected masses. It is a sad but necessary injustice that a repeat of China's historic situation still occurs all over the world, especially in the underdeveloped Third World countries of Asia, Africa, and Latin America. There is a clear and powerful lesson to be learned, but few in power heed it.

Our correspondence and exchange of thoughts on this topic continued into the spring of the following year. We had reached a stalemate but recognized that good will toward the masses was a top priority for all parties involved. In his letter of April 23, 1951, Dr. Pickett concluded our exchange as follows:

> It is doubtful whether . . . [any] purpose would be served were I to undertake a categorical reply to the various points which you have raised in your letters. Upon one thing, of course, you and I can agree personally, and I think all people of good will would so agree. The overwhelming majority of Americans wish for China exactly what you wish for China, namely, years of peace and prosperity during which the nation as a whole can build itself into the great nation which it has been in history, is now, and will be in the future. . . .
>
> Perhaps it could be more simply expressed if one were to say that the overwhelming majority of Americans have been hoping and praying that there could be some way whereby China could get on its feet again, and whereby its peoples could be assured of freedom and peaceful endeavor, without turning the country over either to the reactionaries who surrounded General Chiang Kai-shek, or the Reds who take their orders from Moscow.

The way I saw it, China's situation was unique to China. As history has proved, China did not fall into the manipulative hands of Soviet leaders. It had its own set of problems to be solved through a communism that was adapted to its own needs. With over twenty-five hundred years of a culture based on Confucianism, it would be difficult to imagine that "Chinese" communism could be totally void of some type of moral or ethical base. As I look back even today, I cannot say that the Communist victory of October 1, 1949, was a tragic historical event. True, the people were and still are denied certain freedoms, but people must also have food in their stomachs in order to have the stamina to fight for those very ideals that they hold dear. Nevertheless, what I believed was a solution for China's problems was certainly never my belief or desire for the United States. Unfortunately, this was a point that the United States government failed to understand.

DESCRIPTION

Name - - - CHIN TUNG POK - - - - 2500/10277 - - - -
Age - - 20 - - - Height - - 5 - - ft - - 6 - - - in.
Occupation: - - - - - - - - - Student - - - - - - - -
Admitted as, Son of native, Chin Chu Gin, ex SS - - -
"Evangeline", Boston, Mass., August 5, 1934. - - - -
Physical marks and peculiarities Round pit 1/2" from outer
corner right eyebrow; Line of pits in front of rt ear;
Brown spot center of left upper eyelid; Other marks.
Issued at the port of - - - - - BOSTON, MASS. - - - - -
this - - seventeenth - day of - August - - - 1934.

Immigration Official in Charge

Certificate of Identity
for Chinese Persons,
issued to Chin Tung Pok in
Boston, August 17, 1934

New York, c. 1936

宣誓入伍於紐約美國
第三海軍區司令部
一九四一・十二・廿七日

Swearing-in
ceremony,
U.S. Navy,
December 27,
1941

**UNITED STATES NAVY**
*Identification Card*

CHIN, T. P.
*Name*

*Jung Pok Chin*
*Signature*

Color Hair Black Eyes Brown
Weight 153 Birth 11-10-15
Void after

A. L. KOHR, Lt.
N. Nav. 546   *Validating Officer*

U.S. Navy
identification
card

Iceland, c. 1942, while serving
aboard the *U.S.S. Ranger*

Tung Pok Chin,
Sunday sermon interpreter, with
the Rev. Louis T. Buchheimer,
True Light Lutheran Church,
New York City, 1948

Before leaving for Hong Kong,
in New York City, 1949

Tung Pok Chin marries
Mak Ting Fong,
Hong Kong, 1949

The Brooklyn laundry, c. 1950

Wilson and Winifred Chin
study in the living quarters
behind the laundry, c. 1955

The Chin family at home,
c. 1955

Tung Pok Chin in his study,
after retirement,
Brooklyn, 1978

The fifty-first annual celebration
of the Chinese Hand Laundry
Alliance, New York, 1984
(Chin at far right)

The same celebration, 1984
(Chin facing camera)

Tung Pok Chin reunited with
his son, Wai Yong,
New York, 1986

# Becoming American

# Paranoia

After Dean Pickett's last letter to me in 1951, I was hesitant to continue my correspondence with him for the time being. I noticed that letters I had recently received had been tampered with, as if opened and resealed—and quite sloppily at that!—and I did not want to implicate him in any way by his friendship with me, for this was the beginning of the age of paranoia, and "guilt by association" was rampant. I did not want to cause disruption in anyone's life, much less in the life of a dear friend, so my letter writing ceased, as did my poetry writing. From time to time, however, I did write commentaries on current events as requested by the *China Daily News*.

After my first visit from federal agents in the spring of 1955, I tried to keep a low profile. Wilson had already started kindergarten, and Winifred would start in another two years. Should the current climate persist, I did not want them singled out at school in any way.

I compared my situation with that of the Japanese during World War II. The United States declared war not only on Japan but also on Germany and Italy, yet no German or Italian Americans were rounded up and sent to internment camps. To add insult to injury, many of the elderly Japanese men who were detained during the war had fought for the United States during World War I!

Now, only a few years after the war, I feared that McCarthyism would similarly target the Chinese people because of China's communism. Although many Eastern

European nations had also turned to communism, we Chinese could be set apart by our appearances and by our names, and so, the theory went, one had to be wary of all Chinese.

Our correspondence was now limited to relatives in Hong Kong, to whom we sent annual greetings and parcels of New York souvenirs. We discussed nothing of the ongoing political situation. We in turn received our annual parcels of Chinese-style jackets and other miscellaneous items to which the children looked forward. From time to time we received packages that had been opened and not even resealed, with an explanation that they had been damaged in transport, but I knew that there was more to it than that.

Now, the *China Daily News* ran a column called "Thoughts on Modern Times." This column covered topics ranging from the symbols of celebration for the Chinese New Year to tips on how to complete one's federal, state, and city income tax returns. Others carried news about relatives in mainland China via other relatives in Hong Kong. On this matter there always seemed to be two sides to the story. Refugees from China spoke only of the atrocities of Communist injustice, while the more humble folk who remained talked of the land they were allotted and expressed gratitude for the shirts on their backs and the food on their plates. It was all a matter of perspective.

Thinking to clarify any questionable loyalties of which the United States government had accused me, I voluntarily wrote a commentary on the China situation in the fall of 1955. I cannot recall the exact date when it was published, as I had stopped clipping out my own writings. In this article I referred to the discussion between myself and an anonymous "dean of a major American university." I clearly and logically ran through the argument on both sides of the debate and concluded that we had both desired the same end for China: peace, prosperity, and strength.

Instead of clarifying any misunderstandings, however, I only got myself into hot water. By the winter of 1955 the two agents had returned to my laundry.

"Long time no see, Lai Bing Chan—or Tung Pok Chin," the tall, husky one greeted me.

"Long time no see," I replied in good spirits.

"Yes, you remember us. You don't write much nowadays."

"I don't have the time now. The children are growing and there are more family responsibilities now."

"We have your latest article."

"Good!" I responded.

"You say that everyone wants to see a strong China."

"Yes, that is what I believe."

"You know, China is a communist nation."

"Yes, but I think people would like to see it strong nevertheless, and independent of Soviet domination or influence."

"Oh, I see. So you would like to see China become a strong and independent communist nation."

"I do not mean that it must be a strong communist nation. As long as the people are well fed and have clothing to wear, that is the important thing. That is what a strong nation is—that people should not starve and go naked as I did."

"And you want to see that at all cost?"

"What do you mean?"

"If having what you call a strong nation takes away from free enterprise and the American way of life, would you still believe in it?"

"But I am not speaking for America. I have no complaints about America. I am not trying to change things here, or anywhere. I work hard, but I make a decent living for myself and my family here. In China, even if I worked hard, I still would have nothing! That is the only reason why I say it is good for the farmers now. I know, you think I am a Communist just because I am sympathetic toward hungry people in China. But I am not a Communist, and I am not trying to overthrow the government of the United States! Your accusations are totally unfair!"

I could not help getting excited. I felt they were trying to trick me into saying certain things, and that if I did not watch myself I could be manipulated into admitting to things that were not true. Already we had heard many instances of other paper sons and their families being deported for admitting to communism as a better way of life. To me it was still an open debate, and one in which I took interest only on a philosophical level. After all, it is really a matter of semantics when one considers that even Plato's *Republic,* the first blueprint for democracy, could have been a communist state too. Everyone shared according to his need and gave according to his ability. Even the Bible talked of a community where "as many as were possessors of lands or houses sold them . . . and distribution was made unto every man according as he had need."[1] I did not think that there was anything wrong with what I believed. Besides, I was also interpreter at the True Light Lutheran Church in Chinatown, and every Sunday the entire family went to attend services. Why didn't they take that into consideration?

The two FBI men glanced at each other. My face was boiling red by this time. I had no more to say and neither

---

[1] Acts 4:34–35.

did they. They tipped their hats, nodded to me, and disappeared into the winter chill.

That evening, when Ting Fong returned home from work, I related the incident to her.

"Why did you have to write that article?" she asked.

"It was meant to clarify things."

"Clarify things? What are you trying to do to us?" she burst out.

"How was I to know? I meant well. I wanted everyone to know that we all had China's best interest in mind. That's all the article said."

"Well, you didn't have to say that the farmer in China is better off now because of communism," she retorted.

"I didn't say that he was better off because of communism," I tried to explain. "My point was that as long as he is given the chance to earn a decent living it doesn't matter what you call that government, and that a decent living is what everyone wanted for the Chinese people, Communist or otherwise."

"I don't see why you even had to say that life is better there now."

"Because it is. It's a fact," I insisted.

"Then why don't you go back? Why are you so afraid of being deported?"

"Because I'm already here! I had it bad when I was in China. If I had earned a decent living back home I wouldn't have left. And why should I be forced out now that I'm all settled with a new life and family? I worked hard to get what I have here. I won't give it up now. I fought for this country too, you know. This is my home now!"

"Did you tell them that you were in the U.S. Navy?" she asked with a change in her tone of voice.

"No, but they know all that already."

"Maybe you could mention it to them again."

"Next time," I answered softly.

"Where were the children?"

"They were asleep in the back. The men came early in the morning."

"I don't want them to know about this."

"Don't worry. They'll be fine; everything will be fine."

I could never really understand the accusations of the U.S. government against me. I was hurt. In my heart I felt like an American; America had been my home for over two decades; my children were born here; I served in the U.S. Navy; and I was as patriotic as anyone. Now, because of a few poems and articles, they wanted to deport me. But my worst fear was the possibility that my children would never truly be a part of Gold Mountain. No matter how "American" they were, they too would always look different—Chinese—and be easy to single out. That is why I had started to teach them Chinese. I thought that if the situation ever got too unbearable, then at least they would have the option of "returning" to China when they came of age. They would know Chinese and could be among their own kind. Maybe China would be stronger then, with a better economy, and they could even make a good life for themselves there. As for myself, I had decided at age nineteen that America would be my home despite whatever hardships. Now, I could not even be assured of that.

As we ate dinner that night we mentioned nothing of the day's events. Only Wilson talked about kindergarten and boasted of the new English words he'd learned. He was pitifully comical when he first started school. Since we spoke only Chinese in the home, his English left much to be desired. But children pick up language easily, so I was not overly concerned.

I wrote out four index cards for him to carry on his first day of school. He had to remember that in his front right pocket was a card that read, in large print, *I have to go to the bathroom*. He would show this to his teacher whenever necessary. In his front left pocket was another card reading, *I am feeling ill*. In his back right pocket was the card that read, *Someone hit me*, and in his back left pocket was his identification card with full name, address, and telephone number. Until he could learn these phrases, he carried all four cards daily, each in its respective pocket lest he pull out the wrong one!

By the end of kindergarten he was relatively fluent in English. He hated to see the month of June come to an end because school was such a different experience from home life. Winifred could not wait to start, but she still had another year to wait.

During the summer months the children had more playtime together before their afternoon study of the Confucian classics. The day was more enjoyable and less pressured, and studying into the early evening gave them a chance to wind down by dinnertime. One afternoon, during a Chinese lesson, another two FBI men came by again to observe. They asked if I minded if they stayed a while, and they wanted to see the texts from which I was teaching. Of course I did not mind. I accommodated their needs, allowing them to handle whatever they wanted to see. After listening in on the lesson and flipping through some pages, which were conveniently in both Chinese and English, they seemed satisfied and left.

From the time of my appointment in 1939 as Sunday school interpreter at the True Light Lutheran Church, I had always been a faithful supporter of the church, both financially and in deed. Both of our children were baptized by the Reverend Louis T. Buchheimer, founder and first senior pastor of True Light, and for many years we attended Sunday services together as a family. I never thought to talk to anyone about the problems I was having during this time until close to the end of summer, and considering our sixteen-year relationship I naturally approached the good reverend. After services one Sunday I pulled him aside and informed him of the situation.

"Why should you worry about it?" he asked. "You're a man of fine morals, you're in good standing with this church, you've served your country, and the community thinks very highly of you. You know too that if you ever need a good word, I'm always here for you."

"It helps to know that. I don't worry too much about it. I've seen too much in my lifetime and during the war, and I expect that 'this too shall pass,' as they say. But my wife worries. She doesn't want to be deported and to lose face before her family in Hong Kong. She also worries for the children; she doesn't want them to grow up in this uncertainty and confusion."

"What if you referred these people to me the next time they come by? Maybe it would help if I could talk to them," he offered.

"No, I don't want you to. You would have to lie, and you are a minister. I would not ask that of you."

"Lie about what? Are you a Communist?" he inquired gently. In all the years that I had known Reverend Buchheimer, I had never known him to be anything less than a genuinely sincere and honest man. But I sensed that even if I were a Communist and confessed it to him, he would be protective and say nothing to the authorities to give me away.

"No," I laughed, "I am not a Communist. But you know that I am a paper son."

"Yes, many Chinese men your age and older are paper sons."

"That was the only way we could come to Gold Mountain—to buy our way in."

"All right, I understand," he acknowledged calmly, waiting for the rest of the story.

"Well, those of us from the same village back home still address each other by our true names, not by the names on our papers, so by now everyone in Chinatown knows who I am."

"You're Chin Tung Pok."

"Yes, but Lai Bing Chan to my villagers and when I write poems and commentaries for the *China Daily News.*"

"Oooh, they don't like that paper; they say it has Communist leanings," the reverend warned.

"That's debatable," I maintained. "They report news from the mainland, that's all. And we're not supposed to have any ties with the mainland."

"And you write for them?"

"I only write to amuse myself during the late hours. I admit I am sympathetic to the poor people who have suffered for thousands of years under feudalism and imperial rule, but I am no Communist. I never speak of communism in the church with anybody either. Unfortunately, the United States takes side with the Nationalist government and simply refuses to allow people the freedom of communication. My mail is opened, even letters from relatives in Hong Kong . . ."

"Just in case they have connections with relatives in China," he interrupted.

"My phone is tapped—clicking and static all the time

now. They come to the house whenever they want and just hang around or look through books and magazines. There is prejudice, too! The sanitation men won't collect our garbage if they see Chinese print in the cans when they lift the lids. They just leave it there. We wrap up our Chinese newspapers with American print before discarding them. It makes my wife very uneasy."

"And yourself?"

"Me? I just let them stand there and watch and try to pretend that they are not around. If they ask something, I answer."

"I have heard that you write poetry, and that you're quite talented—they say you focus on 'social concerns,' but I've never heard a bad word said about you. From what I know of you, I do not believe that you are a threat to this country, and I don't see why they are putting you through all this. But given that we are living in an age of political upheaval focused on anticommunism, all I can say right now is that if you know your innocence, then just stick to the facts and they will eventually let you and your family alone. Be cooperative, as you have been, and just keep a low profile by not writing for the time being."

"I've already made that decision."

"Good! Then you have nothing to fear. Mrs. Buchheimer can talk to your wife too and try to put her mind at ease a bit." I had not thought to make that request but was very appreciative of his offer and took him up on it immediately.

"Thank you, thank you," I said, feeling the relief of a great burden being lifted and a large smile spreading across my face. "I'm sure she'll feel better about it too."

"Everything will work out in the end; you'll see." On that note our conversation ended. That same afternoon the reverend asked us to remain in Chinatown until after evening service so that we might dine with him and his family. It was a pleasant surprise and a break from our Sunday routine. We gladly accepted. Our children played together, and the Buchheimers' warmth and hospitality really made us feel welcome again in a country that had been gradually alienating us from the mainstream of society.

# Assimilation

By the fall of 1956, Wilson was no longer a half-day kindergartner but a proud first-grader. He had readers, textbooks, workbooks, notebooks, homework, his own supply of stationery—and a desk at which to work! Winifred, of course, wanted a desk too, so we got her one as well. She would eventually need it anyway.

To keep her busy while her brother and playmate was in school all day, I taught Winifred to play checkers. When business was slow, I played with her. Otherwise she ran to opposite sides of the checkerboard to play against herself. Customers were amazed to see a four-year-old doing this, and occasionally someone would even offer to play with her. Eventually we moved on to Chinese chess, a challenging and highly strategic game similar to chess but played with generals and generals' advisors rather than kings and queens. The soldier on the front line crosses an imaginary river into enemy territory to battle; but unlike the pawn in chess, it cannot be traded in for a more valuable piece once it reaches the opposite end of the board. The soldier in Chinese chess marches on a path of no return.

Several changes took place in the laundry that fall. For one thing, I acted on my wife's suggestion and made a copy of my navy discharge paper, which I framed along with the photo that was taken when I was sworn in—the photo that had appeared in the Chinese newspapers to encourage minority enlistment. I hung these two side by side next to the shelves where the customers' shirts were stacked, right over a bell labeled "ring for service." The bell was needed because during the course of the day I made many trips to the kitchen in the back to fetch pails of water for ironing and starching shirts.

Between the store in the front and the kitchen and bathroom to the rear were three rooms. The five rooms altogether were aligned straight, boxcar style. The first room, our bedroom, was approximately eight by ten feet. All that would fit in it were a large bed and a dresser. A curtain was drawn around our bed, and our daughter slept on a folding cot next to the bed. At night, the cot blocked the doorway between the store and the bedroom, but between the bed and the cot was still a foot and a half of walking space. During the day the cot was folded up.

The next room was even smaller. Six by eight feet, it was barely big enough for Wilson. He had a single sofa bed that he closed every morning before going to school. With it closed during the day, he had a "study" room. Directly opposite the sofa bed was his desk, and right in the middle of the hallway that ran past all five rooms was Winifred's desk. When the sofa bed was opened out, it reached all the way to the desk, and there was not even enough space to open the desk drawers! Still, this sufficed for our growing family for the next ten years.

The third room was our living room. This room was larger, approximately twelve feet by fifteen. In the early days we did not own a television or phonograph, so much of the room was filled with the children's toys; another wall was lined with books. Our only piece of furniture was a couch, for which my wife saved money soon after she started her job at the factory.

Our plans to "redecorate" the quarters were modest. Basically we tried to make the place look as American as possible. We subscribed to *Life Magazine* as well as to the Chinese newspapers, but we discarded the Chinese papers daily and kept only *Life* and a current issue of the *New York Times* for display. We put out some family photos and a picture of me standing beside the Reverend Buchheimer at the altar interpreting a Sunday sermon. We also framed some of Wilson's awards from school.

Life in the fifties was difficult, but the sense of reward for a job well done made it easier. One of the biggest problems in the China I had known was that no matter how hard one worked, hunger was always a fact of life. And having a shirt on one's back in the wintertime was considered a luxury! So it is no wonder that America remained the land of opportunity for so many people.

Ting Fong had been working in the factory for over a year now. In those nonunion days the hours were long and the labor was cheap. She left the house usually around 8:30 A.M. to deliver our son to school by 9:00. She proceeded to Chinatown from there, worked from about 9:30 A.M. until about 7:30 or 8:00 P.M., arriving home for dinner around 8:30 or 9:00. There was no minimum wage then either—everything was paid as "piecework." Many shops in Chinatown still maintain that policy even now. This meant that if a seamstress or machine operator caught on quickly and produced more, he or she got paid more; wages were measured by production. Sometimes, on days when the style was easy and the fabric not too difficult to handle, my wife would work until 10:00 or 11:00 at night, even bringing back "homework" for the weekend. This was illegal then and still is, but it nevertheless still happens because there is a constant influx of new immigrants from Asia who are willing to work hard for a piece of that Gold Mountain dream.

At a time when every penny made a difference, workers often moved from one shop to another for just a few cents more per piece. My wife was one of these workers, and it wasn't long before she had worked in nearly every shop in Chinatown! The shops kept growing, though, and there was always a constant demand for good, fast workers. By the time representatives from the International Ladies Garment Workers' Union[1] started to organize workers from the Chinatown shops, her face was so well known to the organizers that she was nominated as the chairlady of her shop to represent the workers there. She later rose through the ranks to become chairperson of the executive committee of the entire Local 23–25. In fact, she had become so popular with both workers and union negotiators alike that everyone addressed her as "Sister Fong." With the organization of union shops in Chinatown, we gradually saw improvements in working conditions and pay, along with health, retirement, and other benefits previously unheard of.

By the fall of 1957, both children were attending school. Neither had any idea of what McCarthyism was, and although both had been home at various times during visits from FBI men, neither was old enough to understand the exact nature of the visits. To them, they were merely friends dropping by.

Life continued as usual. Ting Fong dropped off the children at school before leaving for the factory, and I picked them up after school. After homework was completed, they had time to play with other children on the block, but they had to return to the laundry at my signal to commence Chinese lessons.

[1] Now merged with the Amalgamated Union to form the Union of Needletrade Industry and Textile Employees (UNITE).

One day, as they were studying the *Analects of Confucius*, I overheard Wilson declare proudly to his sister, "*I'm* important. Two men came to see me at school today."

"They came to see me too," she replied with a spiteful "ha ha."

"No they didn't. They only see *big* people."

"They did too see me . . ." The conversation came to an end when they noticed my glare. Study, after all, was a very serious matter to me, though my shock on this occasion had nothing to do with that, of course. How could anyone send officials into the schools to question such young children, or even possibly try to use their statements against their parents!

"But they didn't talk to you," the teasing continued in a whisper.

"How would you know?"

"Because you're too little."

"That's enough," I interrupted. "Is this how we study? What is the first lesson in the *Analects*?" Together they recited in Chinese, "Confucius said, 'To learn and to practice regularly what has been learned; is this not a pleasure?'" And they continued from there.

The next day I called up the school, PS 116, and asked to speak with the principal. The principal's office received my call and reassured me that no one was allowed to speak with any of the children.

"Our school policy does the utmost to ensure the protection of all children from harassment. You need not worry, Mr. Chin."

"I am only concerned for their well-being. As I explained to you when I first brought our son two years ago to register for kindergarten, we have been the object of investigation by federal agents for several years now. I know my innocence, but I don't want the children to be singled out."

"Please be assured, Mr. Chin. Your children are being treated just like all the other children in school. They are both very bright youngsters, and their teachers are doing all that they can to protect their privacy. They're also very well liked by other children because they're two of a very small minority in the school. They're getting along just fine."

"Did these agents go directly to the children yesterday?" I inquired anxiously.

"No, they didn't. They approached the classrooms and asked permission from the teachers first to speak with each child."

"And how did the teachers respond?"

"According to proper procedure, they asked to what it was in reference—in the event of an emergency. When the men replied that it had to do with immigration papers both teachers decided that it was not a matter in which children their ages would be able to assist, and suggested they question the parents instead."

"Did they leave after that?"

"That's when they approached me, asking if I would intervene on their behalf. I told them 'no' when I questioned them on the subject matter, and explained our school policy to them. They seemed satisfied with that and left quietly."

Throughout the conversation the principal's voice was calm and collected and exhibited no prejudice whatever. I thanked her for her time and concern for the children's welfare, and was thankful that at least the educational branch of our government was protective of the next generation, despite the accusations against the present one. I knew of the other "minority" children the principal had mentioned. They were the Wong children, whose laundry and living quarters had been turned upside down by immigration officials and who had been hounded by the FBI in the middle of the night, and the Gee family, one of whom by a slip of the tongue incorrectly answered a question regarding the number of brothers on his paper; now the whole family faced deportation.

I had known the Wongs since 1950. They were already established in their own business on Central Avenue, and I purchased my laundry just three blocks away with the $300 I had left to my name. He did dry cleaning and I did not, so we established a business relationship whereby he profited from my referrals. Often we met on Sundays and traveled to Chinatown together, and when he discovered that I had taught myself English, he looked on me with great respect as a teacher and advisor. I like to think it was the same type of respect that spared me the humiliation of a violent house search, that perhaps the officers who walked through my door so often sensed that I was different from Mr. Wong or Mr. Gee, because I took the time to learn the English language well enough to communicate and seemed really to want, more than other Chinese immigrants, to assimilate into American society.

On the other hand, I could not deceive myself. I had heard many stories of illegal entries into homes, laundries, and restaurants, and I was aware that my own business and residence might be subject to the same treatment at any time. That possibility never came closer to reality than on the day Mr. Wong called me about the ransacking of his laundry. The phone rang just as I was finishing my lunch in the back of the laundry.

"Teacher," he said, his usual greeting.

"Mr. Wong! How are you? Have you eaten yet?" Chinese conversations, whether in person or by telephone, are unique in that very early on the subject of food will make its way into the talk. This undoubtedly stems from the memory of the Chinese countryside, where so many Chinese go hungry; whenever two or more people meet, food is always the first topic of conversation.

"Fortunately yes, otherwise I wouldn't have the appetite now," he replied in a tense and nervous tone.

"Why? What's the matter?" I was concerned because Mr. Wong was generally a person of good humor and mild disposition. And he had good reason to be content. He and his wife and their son came to the United States in the mid-1930s under one paper in the name of "Lee," satisfactorily answered all questions at the time of immigration, and were able to continue with their lives without disruption. Then two daughters followed—the first generation of native-born Americans! In general, things were good for the Wongs.

"It's hard to explain. Why don't you come over and see for yourself? Can you get away for a few minutes?"

"Of course. I'll see you shortly." I flipped the OPEN sign over to display the reverse, as I did when I closed the shop to pick up the children from school: BACK IN 15 MINUTES.

It was a short enough walk from my laundry to my neighbor's. My laundry was located on Wilson Avenue (originally called Hamburg Avenue but renamed for the twenty-eighth president of the United States after World War II). The Wongs' laundry was located on Central Avenue, just one block away from mine. Both stores were situated between Grove and Linden Streets.

The neighborhood itself was a mixture of Germans, Italians, Irish, and Jews, with just a handful of Asians, including one Japanese family living right across the street from us. Except for a few family storefront businesses, it was basically a residential area. Despite the racial and apparently political and cultural differences, the Bushwick section of Brooklyn was a rather peaceful place in the fifties. Children played together, running and laughing, and everyone supported each other's businesses. There was the linoleum and tile store on the corner of Wilson Avenue and Linden Street, then the grocery store owned by an Italian family next door. The next two houses were equipped with storefronts but businesses were never established; instead, curtains were drawn over the storefront windows and they were used as residences. A candy store owned by a fat Irish couple and another residential storefront apartment followed. Then came the movers, my laundry, a butcher shop, an Italian cheese shop, a dry cleaner, and finally the pool hall on the corner of Wilson Avenue and Grove Street, probably the only "bad element" on the block. Parents used to warn their children to stay away from that corner because it brought teenagers and adolescents in from other neighborhoods to "hang out," blasting the juke box until late at night. The floor plan of all of these houses was more or less identical— storefront, residential space to the rear, and two stories above for leasing. The tallest building was only three stories high, and probably the tallest building in the entire neighborhood was the little redbrick schoolhouse on Knickerbocker Avenue between Grove and Menahan Streets, standing four stories tall.

Mr. Wong's laundry was right across the street from the Children's Health Clinic on Central Avenue. Both of my children went there for their annual checkups. Having all the basic necessities that a community needed, Bushwick, as I recall it, was pretty self-sufficient.

When I arrived at Mr. Wong's I was shocked to see what had happened. I had never seen such a mess!

"See what they did?" Mr. Wong said, slowly shaking his head.

"Who did this?"

"I'm not sure."

"Did they identify themselves? Were they neighborhood kids?"

"Oh, it wasn't kids. They were agents of some sort—with badges. But I didn't really understand what they were saying. They spoke too fast. Just flashed their badges, uttered some phrases nonstop, unlatched the counter, and walked in and started searching. Look—they went through *everything.*" Mr. Wong's laundry had about the same layout as mine. A counter divided the customer side from the work area, and directly behind the counter were wall units with shelves of laundered shirts, all wrapped and arranged by ticket number and ready for pick-up. Opposite the shelves were ironing boards and pressers, and directly to the rear hung all of the dry cleaning. As at my place, dirty laundry was thrown in bulk under the ironing boards until sorted by color, texture, and type. But now everything was all over the floor, all mixed up. Every corner of every shelf, every corner of the floor under the boards, and anything that could be moved had been cleared out as a possible hiding place.

"What were they looking for? I thought your status was fine," I said.

"I thought so too. But you know, I was a paper son. My whole family came under the same paper."

"But you passed interrogations without problems."

"Sure I did. But how many years ago was that? I don't even remember—twenty? Twenty-five? Times have changed," he said, shaking his head once again. "Look at yourself," he continued. "You came to this country in the thirties, too. And you even served in the navy during the war."

"Yeah, it's a shame what one man's ideas of government can do, you know." I had to agree with Mr. Wong. "And this McCarthy fellow was a nobody. That's the scary part!"

"So whatever happened to him?"

"He was denounced. And rightfully so! Thank goodness we had superiors who finally regained control."

"Oh, but they should never have let him get that far to begin with. I mean, look at the Chinese in America now—still living in fear. Of what? Subscribing to the wrong newspaper? You try to buy a product made in China—can you find one?"

"That's another story altogether, though. America recognizes Taiwan as the one legitimate China and will only trade with her." After a slight pause, the conversation went back to McCarthyism.

"When was he denounced?" Mr. Wong asked curiously. He, like many other Chinese people who had no knowledge of English, could go only by the events in their lives to conjecture at what was going on in the country. Many were not literate even in their own language, so they could not read the Chinese newspapers either. Besides, the Chinese newspapers had to be reservedly cautious in writing about this country's affairs during this time, and often the truth never made it into print.

"Oh, back in late 1954," I struggled to recall.

"And here we are in 1957! But you know me, happy-go-lucky. I've done nothing wrong. I was so proud, you know, when our first daughter was born here—right here on Gold Mountain soil!" His eyes filled with tears as he looked back at those precious moments and then looked again at his present surroundings. "What do they think a poor laundry man can do? Do they really think I run a spy network out of this little storefront?"

"No, I don't think they believe that. It's just like you say, that times have changed. Twenty-five years ago China was a free nation. Now, it is communist."

"Well, that doesn't make us Communists!"

"No, but you still have relatives in China, don't you?"

"So what?"

"If you have relatives back home, anything can happen. You might have loyalties to your family; one never knows. What if the government held some family members hostage and demanded information from you about the United States?"

"I'm a laundry man! I'm not a government official; I don't know anything to tell them. Besides, any government that holds my family hostage would be on the raw end of the deal—food and shelter for nothing in return?" he said shaking his head and laughing. "And whose side are you on anyway? Why are you so defensive all of a sudden about what's going on?"

"I'm just trying to look at things from their point of view. It's like the Japanese during World War II. Japan as a nation was the enemy, so the government rounded up the Japanese people in general, just to be on the safe side."

"Very smart," he shook his head. "So detain them all! If you ask me, it's paranoia. And the lives they ruined!"

"You're right. There's no reason for this. Still, my guess is that it will soon be over. I think we're probably feeling the last of the repercussions. It's insecurity. That's all it is. The government just wants to make sure there's no threat to the nation."

"Well, I hope you're right. Come, take a walk through the back." Like us, the Wongs used the rear of the laundry for their living quarters. When he led me through the rooms, it was an even worse mess. Their clothing, letters, papers, photos, the girls' schoolwork, and possessions from China and Hong Kong had all been rummaged through and scattered all over the place. Desks and dressers had been emptied, drawers turned over, and linen strewn everywhere in disarray.

I invited Mr. Wong back to my laundry to get away from the situation for a while. We took tea together and chatted some more until school let out.

"You're lucky," he remarked as he glanced around at the meticulously kept shelves of bundled shirts. "They don't bother you—or do they?"

"Oh, they come around but mostly we just talk. So I guess I've gotten away comparatively easy, at least so far," I said, keeping my fingers crossed. This ubiquitous "they" in any general conversation gradually came to mean the entire category of FBI men, Immigration and Naturalization officials, and any other interrogators lumped into one.

"Do they ever come in?"

"Sure. They look around. Sometimes they just watch. I try to pay them no mind. If I am working, I continue to work, and I don't say a word until they start up. The last time they came I was in the middle of a Chinese lesson with my children. They asked to look at the text I was using, so I let them look at it. Then they left."

"That's all?"

"It's against the law to just walk in and start searching, you know. They need a search warrant for that. They know that."

"Of course they know! But maybe it's because they know that you know it too that they don't trespass on your territory. You could really write them up and give them a bad name."

"No, I'm staying away from that for now. The last time I wrote an article to clear myself of any suspicions I only made things worse. I just try to get on with everyday living now."

"What about your children?"

"They're young; they'll be fine."

"Don't you want them to grow up in a more stable environment?"

"Sure, but what can I do? Where would I go? I can make a decent living here and support my family. You know that, that's why we're here. Besides, the peasant farmers may be better fed and better clothed now, but who knows how long that will last? The Chinese Communist government is only eight years old right now as we speak. Who knows what will happen there another eight years from now? I won't uproot my family to return to an uncertain situation either. We've both made our homes here."

It was time to pick up the children. As we walked out the door together I assured Mr. Wong that things would settle down in time, difficult as it seemed at the moment to believe.

The fall of 1957 marked a new beginning for all of us, as Wilson entered a new phase of cultural learning and assimilation into American society. I can never forget the day he came home from school with a plate of turkey and a note from his second-grade teacher, reading:

Dear Mr. Chin,

Having learned that you are not familiar with our Thanksgiving tradition, I am sending your son home with a few slices of turkey for sampling. I hope that you and your family will enjoy these cuts. Happy Thanksgiving.

Sincerely, Mrs. ——

"How did this come about?" I asked curiously.

"When we all went back to school after the long weekend, the teacher asked how many children had turkey for Thanksgiving. Everyone raised their hands except me, so she looked at me and said, 'You didn't have turkey?' I said, 'No.' Then she asked if I ever had turkey, and I told her again, 'No.' Then she smiled and said, 'Okay, we'll take care of that.'"

I felt both embarrassed and saddened that my son was the only child in the class who did not have turkey on this all-American holiday, but was glad that his teacher was understanding and sensitive enough to introduce us to a taste of American tradition.

"That was very thoughtful of her," I said, though in fact I was more concerned with the way Wilson might have felt at being singled out in class. The last thing I wanted him to feel was deprivation, of which I myself experienced enough growing up in China. I searched his face, but he did not seem to be embarrassed or troubled by the incident. "We'll eat this tonight and you can tell her tomorrow how much we all enjoyed it."

The next day I sent Wilson off to school with a little note of thanks for the initiation into the "American way of life." We actually found turkey to our liking and, since it was the American thing to do, we ate turkey every Thanksgiving from that year on!

Winter eased in as the remains of 1957 were slowly buried in the snow. In the chilly months we kept warm by eating around the dinner table in a Cantonese cooking style called *da bien lo*. Here, all the meats and vegetables are cut up into thin slices, just enough for one mouthful, and set on the table raw. A huge electric cooker is placed at the center of the table, and in it slowly boiling water is seasoned with soy sauce, oyster sauce, sesame seed oil, and a host of other Cantonese flavorings. Each one of us had his bowl of rice in front of him, the only precooked item on the table. The meats and vegetables were then picked up one piece at a time with chopsticks, dipped into the boiling water until desirably cooked, and then eaten with the rice. If our hands and fingers were cold, we held them over the steam from the boiling water to warm them up, then placed our hands on our equally chilled faces and closed our eyes to imagine ourselves basking in the sun somewhere; it was the Chinese equivalent of a warm, cozy fireplace!

Conversations at the dinner table at this time of year usually centered around what exotic goodies the children would receive from Hong Kong for Christmas. We also argued over what would be the most appropriate American gift to send to relatives there. In addition, there was the annual exchange of photos with the various uncles, aunts, and cousins, and the marveling and "oohs" and "aahs" over how much everyone had grown.

We received our correspondence from Hong Kong as usual this year, but in contrast to previous years, I noticed that the letters were all intact; and grandmother's parcel was so neatly wrapped! We had grown so accustomed to having everything opened and scrutinized and then thrown together again haphazardly that receiving "normal" mail was truly a pleasant surprise.

Christmas was one of the children's favorite holidays, second only to the Chinese Lunar New Year. Not only did they enjoy looking at family photographs together and exchanging and opening gifts from family, but there were also the visiting and dinner invitations from new friends made at Sunday school. My children felt particularly proud of the fact that their father was the church and Sunday school interpreter, and their peers always envied them the privileged status this gave them. "Here come Pastor Lai's children," they would say in jest, but never disrespectfully or mockingly. Christmas was also the time when we cleaned out our closets to give old clothes and toys away to the needy. This, to the children, meant that newer garments and games were coming, so they were always generous in ridding themselves of their old possessions.

We usually kept our tree until the first weekend of the New Year. Christmas would not come again for another eleven and a half months, and it no longer made sense to have a tree in the home when the holiday was so far away! My wife and children always had the joy of decorating it, as well as the sadness of taking everything apart. A solemn air would pervade the house a day or two before the dismantling, in stark contrast to the cheer that reigned when we stayed up late on New Year's Eve to watch the festivities in Times Square on television.

# The Homecoming

With 1957 exiting so smoothly, 1958 was sure to bring good tidings. Early one afternoon in the spring of 1958, we received a telephone call from B7.

"Brother-in-law! Guess who this is?" His voice had changed dramatically since we had last spoken, when he was a child running from Immigration to protect his "paper" relatives. He spoke with such command now! I would hardly have known that this was the same person, except that we had been expecting to hear from him, knowing that his discharge was approaching. Besides, I had only one brother-in-law here in the United States! Given the climate of McCarthyism, we had agreed in advance to have no contact during B7's years away in the service. Hearing his voice on the telephone gave my spirits an instant lift, and all of a sudden I felt like the family had been reunited, as indeed it had been. I had not been so excited since my reunion with my own father here in Gold Mountain over twenty years before.

"B7? Is it really you? Are you back for good?"

"You bet! I'm not only honorably discharged, but I made a confession and I'm now a free man in my own proper name again," he proudly declared.

"That was the best thing you could have done. I told you right, then, eh?" I said, laughing heartily away. "No one chasing you around any more, right?"

"Not a soul—what a relief! And in five years, I'll be eligible for naturalization as an American citizen!" In the excitement in his voice one could still sense a trace of the adolescent, but then he had lost most of his adolescence to running scared, and there was much to be made up for.

"We must see you soon. Where are you now?"

"I'm staying at the 'Y' again—just like in the old days. In fact, not too far from you. I'm near Prospect Park."

"Fine, then you'll come over for dinner; come now," I urged him. I was anxious to cut the conversation short and have him here in person instead. I had not yet prepared the meal for the evening, so I quickly called Ting Fong at the shop and asked her to bring extra food from Chinatown for the occasion. She brought home a feast.

It did not take long for B7 to appear at our laundry and, to my surprise, he arrived in full uniform. What a cause for celebration! He walked through the door and straight up to the counter with a big grin stretched across his face. The children, who had just set out their Chinese books on the table next to the ironing board to commence their lessons, looked up, then looked at each other, wondering and whispering to each other about who this stranger might be. It finally dawned on Wilson as this soldier removed his army hat that he had a familiar face. Winifred, however, was at a complete loss. She had been barely three years old when he enlisted and had no recollection at all of the face.

"You know who I am?" B7 asked the children.

"You're . . . uh . . . you're B7!" Wilson cried out.

"Hey, you remember B7!" he replied. Suddenly there was a silence in the air, very solemn, and I was sure that B7 was thinking what I was: that my children had never once addressed him as "uncle." No, they did not know; they could not know that we were related. And now, when they were the tender ages of eight and six, it was still not the proper time to explain these things. He would have to remain B7 to them until they grew old enough to understand.

One thing about Chinese relations is that they are very specific. In contrast to American society, where the term "uncle" is used quite freely (even friends of the family are often addressed by children as "uncle" so-and-so), Chinese terms for brothers, sisters, aunts, uncles, cousins—even grandparents and cousins of parents—all depend on whether the relative is older or younger than oneself or one's parents, and on whether the relative is related on the maternal or paternal side of the family. Thus, even grandparents have separate ways of being addressed depending on whether they are maternal or paternal grandparents. Likewise, there is no straightforward term for "cousin." Cousins are addressed by a term that automatically reveals whether that cousin is male or female, older or younger than the addressee, and stems from the maternal or paternal side of the immediate family. So it is with all terms of address within the immediate and extended family. It is a very complicated structure, but it all reveals the importance of respect for age and status within the Chinese family.

"Come in, come in," I motioned, as I was ironing a shirt. "Your sister will be home soon. Make yourself comfortable." I glanced over to the children, both anticipating my nod of approval to put away their books on this special occasion. "Okay, no Chinese lesson today. Go and play," I conceded. Both packed away their books in record time, but playing was not the first thing on their minds. They dragged B7 back out of the store and paraded him down the block, eager to show him off to their friends in his uniform. And their friends were indeed impressed. Little children looked up at him, asked who he was, where he'd been, and so forth. To the little kids on the block, B7 was a man of the world! After parading him around, they led him back to the laundry, making sure their friends knew that this man in uniform was connected to their household. They certainly were proud of him! They then proceeded to lead him to the back of the laundry, gathering up their toys. B7 followed them to the rear, dragging with him the huge duffel bag in which his few personal belongings were packed, along with a host of gifts and souvenirs from Europe. But before he could even set his bag down, the children grabbed him by the hands, one on each side, led him to a juvenile dinette set in the corner of their play area, and served him candy, bubble gum, and soda from a miniature hostess tea set. Imagine the look on my wife's face when she returned home to see her twenty-one-year-old brother laughing and playing along, just like a child, being entertained by children!

We literally had years to catch up on. I closed shop early for the day so that we could enjoy more hours together, although shop was never really "closed." For whatever shirts remained unpressed or unsorted at the end of each evening would have to be pressed, sorted, and wrapped up in the wee hours of the next morning. Such was life in Gold Mountain.

Dinner that night consisted of chicken, roast duck, lobster Cantonese style, and a mixed assortment of Chinese vegetables. We feasted until late, listening to tales of B7's army experiences, his adventures and travels, and of the friends he made during his time away. We were especially concerned about whether he had encountered any racial prejudices or political problems because of McCarthyism at home.

"No one dared to pick on me. They all thought I knew kung-fu," he laughed.

"Really? Did you study kung-fu?" the children wanted to know.

"No, not me," he replied, shaking his head. "They taught us self-defense in basic training, but that was as close as I got."

"Then how'd you fool everybody?"

"I did pretty well, so everyone assumed I had a background."

"You did well? Will you show me something?" Wilson asked, anxious to learn.

"Another day, all right? We just ate. Here, why don't you feel my muscles," B7 said, changing the subject. "You know, I worked out every day," he said as he rolled up his sleeves and showed off his muscles, first one arm, then the other. As the children satisfied their curiosity with punches and pinches to their uncle's arms, my wife and I gazed at him with astonishment at how much he had changed, both physically and emotionally. B7, the "seventh baby," had grown up, and we could hardly get over it.

Soon after the dinner table was cleared, B7 took out the huge duffel bag and showed us his collection of army medals and insignias, along with a collection of souvenirs ranging from empty bullet shells to a magnificent cutlery set with etched blades and hand-carved ivory handles that he had purchased while stationed in Germany.

"This is for you," he said, handing us the cutlery. It was so regal and imposing that no one in his right mind would decline it. But although anyone would have gladly accepted and cherished it, it was simply too much for us.

"No, no," my wife resisted, "we can't take that."

"No," I added, "you save that for yourself—for when you have a family of your own."

"But I want you to have it. I bought it with you in mind . . ."

"No," I said firmly. "Now that you're out of the army you have a world ahead of you. You'll finish your education, get a good job, get married, and have a fine home and family of your own someday. Take your time. Don't give us the best right away. We have no use for something this beautiful anyway. And your future will surely be brighter than ours."

"But of course you can use it. You could have used it tonight, too, with all the food we had."

"No, you take it with you. This is too good to be wasted on us," I insisted. Modesty and humility have always been traits of the Chinese people, and to some degree my refusal to accept this gift stemmed partially from that tradition. But I also genuinely felt that it was beyond me, recalling how I had grown up in the back country of China and reflecting on our present living conditions in a laundry. What need did we have of such fine wares?

"All right, all right," B7 finally gave in, "you don't have to accept it, but you keep it for me. I don't trust the room at the 'Y.' It's not permanent and the locks are not the most secure." I looked at my wife, and she consented to the idea.

"Fine. We'll hold it for you then. But as soon as you settle down, you take it back for yourself," I repeated.

"All right, don't worry," B7 motioned with his hand to stop the bickering. Case closed, we moved on to dolls and toy guns, how the children would divide the emptied bullet shells between themselves, and other matters of greater importance. Wilson had a special fondness for the insignia with the crossed rifles, and Winifred conveniently preferred the ones with the raised initials "U.S." on them.

Having divided up the spoils, the children were off to bed. My wife brought out Chinese pastries along with Oolong tea, and we chatted into the night. B7 wanted to know if I ever got into trouble for covering up for him, and we were all able to look back and laugh as I recalled the time I sent the immigration officials on a wild goose chase to a former address in New Jersey. We filled him in on life under McCarthyism, and he in turn talked about life in the military. When we had exhausted the subject of the past, we moved on to the present. The present to me, of course, meant getting a good education, without which the future would only be limited.

"So, what is your next step now?" I asked.

"Next step? Get a job," he shrugged. "What else?"

"You could go back to school," I suggested.

"No, it's too late. I can't sit still and study now, after seeing all the action I've seen in the past few years."

"You're only twenty-one. You're still of college age."

"But I didn't even finish high school. It's just too late. Besides, I was never the studying type. Older brother used to get angry at me for not spending more time with my head in the books. He spanked me too sometimes." The older brother, of course, was the senior medical student at the time of B7's arrival in the United States. Now a successful physician with his own clinic on Hong Kong's fashionable Nathan Road, he still wrote letters to his youngest brother to encourage him to return home and continue his schooling. And so we discussed that too.

"You know, it would not be so bad if you returned to Hong Kong now. It certainly would be easier as far as language is concerned. And with your brother's offer to put you through college, you would have a much brighter future there."

"Return to Hong Kong? *Now?*" B7 was startled that I would even suggest the possibility, but I thought for certain that it must have crossed his mind before. It certainly had when he first arrived in this country!

"Why not?" I asked. "I thought you didn't like it here."

"I didn't. But that was when I first got here."

"But if you remain here without completing your education, you'll just end up doing the same thing you did before."

"It's different now. I was a child then; I was idealistic. Now I can accept the situation as a fact of life. I've matured."

"I don't doubt that, but you are still a child in many ways. You've never worked here before, except underground while running from immigration. Now that that's out of the way, it doesn't mean that Gold Mountain is going to blossom for you. And you mustn't accept restaurant labor as a fact of life. The truth of the matter is that life can be better, either here or back in Hong Kong. But you must return to school. Trust me. I'm old enough to be your father. And if I were your age now, I would do it myself."

"But I don't mind restaurant work. It's an honest living—and this time no one will be chasing after me."

"But you can do better! What's a few years' time spent in learning when you have a lifetime of work ahead of you?"

"Brother-in-law," he said shaking his head hopelessly, "it's just that I never enjoyed school or studying, and I know that I won't like it now either. That's why I left home at fifteen to come here—I was anxious to seek my fortune, and I absolutely refused to study back home. I was very difficult for everybody—refused to cooperate, went on a hunger strike, did everything to make everyone miserable until they gave in and agreed to let me come here."

"But you have also discovered by now that there are no such things as streets paved with gold, and no overnight fortunes."

"I know," he said with his head bowed and voice silencing as he spoke.

"And you are willing to settle for a life of restaurant work?"

"I've already accepted it. Many Chinese people here do. It's no shame. It doesn't carry the same stigma here that it does back home, so if that's what I choose to do, then I'm better off doing it here. That's how I look at it." Restaurant workers in China have traditionally been considered the lowliest of workers. To have to bow down and serve food to others is a humbling acknowledgment that one can do no better in life, and only those who were not successful in their studies would do such work. In the United States, however, it seems common enough, and is often seen as one of the few options for the non-English-speaking immigrant. In this way, B7 was right; here, it is no shame and carries no connotations of failure.

"It's hard work, waiting on tables all day," I said.

"I know, but I'm prepared to accept it."

B7's decision was respected. He obtained a job quickly enough and eventually worked his way up to be a head-waiter and bartender, finally saving enough money to buy into another restaurant as a partner.

After five years B7 became a naturalized American citizen. We returned to the laundry after attending the swearing-in ceremony to share in the cutting of a cake, appropriately decorated with red, white, and blue icing in the image of the United States flag. Later that same year, 1963, he married and started a family. His mother, the poised, dignified Chinese lady with the gold-rimmed glasses who dressed as a country peasant woman to accompany her son to the U.S. General Consulate in Hong Kong for questioning, came for the wedding. Arriving with joy at the sight of her youngest "baby" getting married, she left with tears overflowing that she had unwittingly destined her son to a life of restaurant work.

As is true for all those who do not take advantage of a formal education, time and experience become the best teachers. In time, B7 did admit that returning to school would have made life much easier. Nevertheless, his dream of success in Gold Mountain eventually materialized through his children: All three attended and graduated from top universities in the northeastern United States, with careers in engineering, computer science, and pharmacy, and all have families of their own now.

B7 and his family became regular visitors to our home, and although he promised at each visit to take back the set of knives that he brought over from Germany, he never followed through. They were always too much trouble to carry, and there was always "next time."

# The Problem with Confessing

The year 1958 did indeed bring all of the good things we had hoped for and expected. It was a jovial year, and with B7's confession and homecoming we were truly a family again with nothing to hide. His confession, in fact, led my wife and me to consider seriously whether we would benefit from doing the same, although she was more enthusiastic than I.

"Why not?" she asked. "Look at my brother now. He has no one after him anymore." However, I saw things differently.

"The only problem with making a confession now," I said, "is that we would be stripped of all citizenship privileges for the next five years until we could become naturalized again. It's a very slow process, you have to understand that. Also, your brother was being chased around because he falsely answered some very vital questions regarding his paper, and immigration officials knew that he was not whom he claimed to be."

"Then what about our identities? And the children's names? And the generations after that? Our name is not Chin."

"But what name would I confess to? Chin is not my real name, but neither is Lai. Mr. Lai was a Gold Mountain man himself who left his wife back home with no family. That is why they purchased me from the bandits. You know that."

"Well, you can still confess to the name Lai. After all, they did raise you as their own." My wife wanted to live in Gold Mountain as legitimately as possible, which was quite understandable for someone who arrived in the United States only in 1950, just in time to experience the onslaught of McCarthyism. In this matter I could not blame her. But I had my own legitimate concerns too.

"Lai is the name I do my writing under. Lai is the man the government is suspicious of, remember? Now I should embrace that name officially? Besides, the way I see it, neither name is truly my own," I said, sticking to my point. That was the only reason why I had never confessed. "What's the point of confessing when I don't even know what my real name or date of birth is? Anyway, there are more important things to consider when you willingly give up citizenship for a five-year period," I tried to explain.

"What could be so important that could not wait five years? The children are young, and we are not going anywhere." It took a bit of thought, but after a while I came up with a more compelling objection.

"Suppose your mother or one of your siblings wanted to come to the United States in a few years' time," I said. "You cannot sponsor anyone unless you are a citizen. If we confess now, we would have to wait; then they have to wait. It will be years before anyone can come."

"They all have good professions in Hong Kong. Why would they want to come here anyway? To be waiters and laundry men?"

"You have to look beyond that. Don't you see? Even if they are doing well in Hong Kong now, who knows what will happen in the years to come? In 1997 Hong Kong and Kowloon will be returned to the Chinese government and they will be living under a communist regime. I know it seems like a long way off, but that's less than four decades away. This is only 1958, but think—you've been here almost a whole decade already! Time passes quickly. People may panic with the turn of 1960 and everyone may suddenly want out as time runs low. Remember, the U.S. government imposes a very strict quota on immigrants from Hong Kong too. The waiting list will be so long by then that the doors may be closed by the time their turn comes around. There will be no way you can get them out then."

"That's true," she agreed with a nod of the head. "I'm surprised they haven't mentioned anything about it in their letters."

"Perhaps not yet, but you can be sure that they will eventually. It is easy not to think of the imminent when things are going well. But as the twenty-five or thirty-year mark approaches, some journalist may report on the future of Hong Kong as a communist state. A series of articles like that can lead to mass panic and exodus. With a bit of foresight, the next few years might be a better time to consider emigration just to stay ahead of the crowd."

My wife acknowledged the point and said nothing further. While the idea of confessing came up again occasionally, we could agree on no specific, practical advantages in it. We did agree, however, that losing the privileges of citizenship for five years would certainly be a disadvantage should a situation arise in which we needed them. After thoughtfully weighing the pros and cons of it all, confession didn't seem to matter much anymore, and the idea was eventually dropped.

In the meantime, Chinese newspapers all over the country encouraged paper sons and their families to come forth and confess, giving assurances that they would not be deported or prosecuted. But in spite of these appeals, many still feared deportation. Immigrants who managed to buy their way into Gold Mountain had worked hard all their lives to make a decent living. They'd lived under false names from the outset and were very well aware that the Immigration and Naturalization Service knew it, too. But so long as most Chinese immigrants fit the "black hair, black eyes" and "no distinguishing birthmarks" description and answered all of the background questions correctly, there was nothing the government could do but grant them entry.

What did they really stand to gain by confession? And what if confession turned out to be a trick? What if paper sons and daughters confessed to entering the United States under false pretenses and were sent back to China? These concerns were not without foundation. Life was difficult enough in China in the old days, and it still is. That's why we came to Gold Mountain. But as difficult as things were before the revolution, at least in those days one could send money back home and know that the family was well provided for; one could even dream of someday retiring back home with a modest Social Security payment, which when converted to the Chinese *yuan* would have impressed any big-time spender, even in Shanghai!

Now, however, we could no longer communicate freely with relatives in Communist China, especially since McCarthyism. Nor could we be sure that relatives there freely spoke their minds in letters to us. So who was to say that money sent back home actually reached the families? A check freely deposited to the Bank of China was not necessarily as freely withdrawn in China. And indeed, there were reports that money sent home never reached its intended recipients, but whether this was true or merely Nationalist or U.S. propaganda we could not know for sure.

Thus, in spite of the reports that life had improved for Chinese peasant farmers under communism, no one wanted to be deported. That was what prevented most Chinese from confessing. And so the dream of returning to the homeland in old age also died with the revolution. Perhaps it is because we have all dug too hard in these mountains here looking for gold to want to give it up at this point. Whatever the reasons, I sympathized with the fears of other paper sons about the prospect of confessing.

And yet, with more and more reports of paper sons gradually coming forth each day to confess, there developed a renewed faith and confidence in the United States government, and the paper status was slowly becoming a thing of the past. Of course, for most paper sons, there were distinct advantages to confessing and becoming a citizen in one's rightful name, the foremost being that one could eventually sponsor one's own parents and siblings to come to the United States. In my case, however, there were no immediate relatives I wished to bring over here. As for my wife, she was already naturalized, and her immediate family bore the same name as her true maiden name, so no conflict of interest existed. It seemed to us that the risks of confession outweighed the benefits, and so we left it at that.

# The Final Visit

On January 12, 1959, two FBI agents returned to my laundry on Wilson Avenue in Brooklyn. They were not the same ones who had come in previous years, but they were similar in appearance. The tall, husky officers stood on the opposite side of the street, watching. When they saw me come to the front of the store from the rear with a bundle of shirts in my arms, they came hurriedly across the street and opened the door.

"You are a citizen," one of them said, "Tung Pok Chin?"

"Yes."

"Any proof?" I laid the shirts down in a laundry basket on the floor and produced a photocopy of my discharge paper from the United States Navy. They inspected it carefully. "What is your father's name?"

I was really taken aback this time. I never expected them to come out and ask me this question. After all, it had been twenty-five years since the initial interrogations at Boston, and I had entirely forgotten my paper father's name. To gain time, I lifted the laundry basket to the ironing board, huffing and puffing each step of the way, slowly removed the top shirt for pressing, and then straightened out my own shirt and collar before answering them. It took me a few minutes to recall his name, but it finally came to me.

"Chin Chu Gin." We Chinese from the old country place our surnames first, as is still the case. My name then, in traditional Chinese structure, would be Chin Tung Pok. But in time I adapted to placing Chin last, as is the custom in America.

126

"How many times have you been married?"

"Once," I replied indifferently. They smiled.

"Are you a member of the Chinese Hand Laundry Alliance?"

"Yes."

"It is a pro-Communist organization. Why did you join it? You don't have to. You understand English."

"I am a laundry man. In case of trouble with customers I don't have to look for a lawyer elsewhere."

"You want to quit it?"

"No," I said casually.

"Why not? You can join the other one."

"I don't like the other one. This one services better."

"You write poems, right?"

"Yes."

"Does anybody else write using your name?"

"Oh, I don't know."

"Why do you send your poems to the *China Daily News*?"

"I want to make a name as a poet."

"You could send it to the Nationalist paper."

"I don't like the Nationalist paper. This one covers the news more objectively."

"You wrote something against the United States." This was a false accusation. I had written of homesickness, of Chinese immigrant life here in Gold Mountain, of events abroad, and of struggles, triumphs, and tragedies in everyday human existence, but never anything against the United States. So I answered confidently, "Never."

"We have clippings of all your poems."

"Good."

"Do you make contributions to the *China Daily News*?"

"Every year."

"How much?"

"Only a few dollars."

"Why do you make contributions to a Communist paper?"

"They have no money and they asked for help."

"Would you make any contributions to *Life Magazine*?" one of the agents asked as he flipped through the pages of a copy of the magazine on the counter top.

"I would, but they never asked for help."

"You should stop reading the *China Daily News*."

"Why? I read all kinds of papers and magazines, as long as they report the facts. I read the *New York Times* too. I am a poet, and I need material. If you don't want anyone to read it you can close it down."

At this point one of the agents unlatched the hook under the counter top, crossed over to my work area, and entered the back room, where I kept many books, magazines, and writing materials. He looked around casually and finally focused on one book.

"May I look at this?" he asked politely.

"Sure." He removed one volume of a pocket-sized Confucian classic from the shelf and studied it for a while before replacing it.

"How did you learn English?" The questions they asked were never coherent. By asking random questions here and there they hoped to break my own train of thought and to catch any inconsistencies more easily.

"I'm self-taught. I am a Sunday school interpreter in church." In a moment of pride I made a slip of the tongue, volunteering information they had not asked for. I saw my mistake at once. I did not want to drag others into this investigation and risk having to explain any possible conflicting stories.

"Which church?"

I went about my work and pretended that I had not heard the question. I did not answer them, and they did not press further for a reply.

"Your name is Tung Pok Chin, eh? Or maybe Lai Bing Chan?"

I grinned, and they went out laughing and shaking their heads. They never returned again. Perhaps they finally realized that I was just a harmless poet trying to make a living for my family here in Gold Mountain.

# Writing Again

Years of not writing were difficult; many feelings were suppressed. Finally, when my friend Reverend Buchheimer informed me that he was leaving the True Light Congregation for missionary work in the Philippines, my heart was heavy with sorrow. It was 1959.

Late that year I resumed writing again. After the FBI men had come and departed so harmlessly, I made a conscious effort to keep all subject matter as neutral as possible. My first poem was "To the Reverend Buchheimer upon His Departure from True Light Lutheran Church":[1]

> My heart ached on learning that you had accepted another
>     call—
> I can still remember interpreting Sunday Sermons for you at
>     the altar;
> You came to our community, a Pastor kind and giving,
> And founded the congregation that is True Light.
> I thought to say farewell by the traditional breaking of a
>     willow branch,
> But at the time of your departure I was paralyzed with sorrow;
> Our twenty-year friendship is like an ever-flowing stream of
>     water;
> It is unbearable as I turn to watch the river flow east.[2]

[1] The Reverend Louis T. Buchheimer was the founder and first senior pastor of True Light Lutheran Church, located at 195 Worth Street (corner of Mulberry and Worth Streets) in New York's Chinatown. Reverend Buchheimer left for the Philippines in the fall of 1959 after accepting a call there for Lutheran missionaries. The poem was written in memory of the years we spent working together, from 1939 to 1959.

[2] In Chinese tradition, a river flowing eastward is symbolic of great sorrow.

After publishing a few poems and essays sporadically over the next few years, my writing career was given new life. It was just as suddenly cut short again, however, when Wilson entered college in 1967 and chose to major in aeronautical engineering. I stopped writing for fear that because of my background he would be denied security clearance in the event he wished to go into government service. He did work briefly one summer at the Point Mugu Naval Missile Base in California and had no problems, but after graduate school he opted for what turned out to be a very a successful career in private industry. I was thankful that my questionable loyalties did not affect his status, and I also felt that the government was more than fair to him.

By 1970 we were again in the public eye, only this time in a much more pleasant light. My wife, who had worked her way through the ranks of the ILGWU from chairperson of her shop to chairperson of the executive board, was singled out to be interviewed by Bernadine Morris of the *New York Times.* On January 4, 1971, a family photo of us appeared on the front page of the metropolitan section with an interview about her life as a seamstress, in which she compared the days before the union to life and benefits afterward. The ILGWU Local 23–25 paper reprinted the article for members. We were all very proud and felt very American.

That fall Winifred entered college and majored in philosophy. Soon afterward I safely resumed writing again. By then, President Nixon had gone to China, diplomatic ties with the mainland had been reestablished, and trade had resumed. In 1975, when my daughter took a graduate course in contemporary Chinese poetry at Seton Hall University, she brought home two mimeographed poems that the professor had handed out to the class, introducing them as written by the "contemporary Chinese poet" Lai Bing Chan. The first touched on the dreams and harsh realities of immigrant life:

> Immigrants from China one by one
> Arrive in Gold Mountain bringing daughters and sons;
> With joyous hearts they face new life,
> But soon start sinking in the daily strife;
> How rare is that harmony they used to know!
> Filial piety and the Book of Rites[3] are no longer followed;
> For the greatest pleasure now is the rendezvous
> To the track for an up-date on the race horse news.

The second dealt with the feelings of families left behind:

> Upon hearing that his son had reached Gold Mountain,
> The country elder was happy and relieved;
> For he knew that his debts would soon be reduced,
> But a glorious return is not easily attained!
>
> Many a worker has been buried in the dust,
> Struggling for years to barely survive;
> While the wife back home regrets the loneliness she must live
> In exchange for American dollars and Gold Mountain lust.

I was honored that my work was finally being read at the university and accepted as "contemporary poetry" instead of just the writings of a would-be poet with communist leanings. That was all I wanted.

Encouraged by my new status among the intellectuals, I continued to write. My decision to stick to neutral subject matter guided my theme in "Reminiscing on the Old Country at Springtime":

---

[3] One of the "Five Classics" that form the classical Confucian education, the other four being the Book of History, the Book of Poetry, the Spring and Autumn Annuals, and the Book of Changes.

After fifty years in Gold Mountain,
I dream of the woods and streams of the old country:
Orchids blooming in green pastures waft their fragrances afar
As birds announce the Springtime anew with songs in Sha-tou
   Village;
The hazy shadows of geese in the pond reveal a dim sunlight,
But a clear sky shows forth as clouds slowly disperse;
In the days to come, when there is a chance to meet the old
   folks,
I wish to write poems to fully describe the country scene.

I also wrote about the 1980 eruption of Mount St. Helen:

The volcano erupted, proclaiming glory with ashes a-flying;
Everywhere, people fled for their lives.
After all, nature is superior to all mankind,
And would not allow science to be called the pride of heaven!

However, with the reestablishment of diplomatic ties between the United States and China still at such an early and crucial stage, I could not keep the political streams of consciousness from somehow drifting to surface. Thus, when Ronald Reagan was elected president that same year, I wrote "Pondering World Peace":

Peace is in the hands of the United States and China;
Existing together we share the benefits worldwide.
So will President Reagan, once wearing the actor's mask,
Now bring forth universal harmony?

I occasionally allowed myself to become more daring when I read of positive developments in China, especially in the back country. I so often recalled the days of sickness and cold with no doctor available within miles, that when I read of the so-called "barefoot doctors" of the 1960s being sent by the government to help the sick in the countryside, I immediately composed "In Praise of Barefoot Doctors":

Divine healers are of the days of old,
Not to be found in the modern world;
In the countryside the sick prayed to the gods for protection
As the penniless dead were wrapped in grass mats to be
    buried.

Such things as we have seen were commonplace;
What can one say, looking back through ancient eyes?
Now there arises in the new republic government
Barefoot doctors throughout the countryside!

Likewise I took a chance and expressed my pride in China's military and infrastructure with "The Great Yangtze River Bridge":

A great bridge crosses the Yangtze River;
Chungking, Nanking, and Wuhan are proudly united.
What forces can oppose us if we stand together?
Amid adversities a union of strength triumphs all.

On the railing I watch the banks of the Great Yangtze;
Warships of a thousand masts are pleasing to the eye;
Absorbed in a military display of might
I suddenly notice the effortless beauty of an adjacent pond.

But mostly I kept my promise to myself to remain neutral in my themes, as in "On Writing Poetry":

Why use intricate clauses in writing poetry?
Simplicity that cleanses the heart is my teaching;
Though Po Chu-yi[4] of the T'ang Era was never so complex,
His Song of Unending Sorrow has triumphed over a thousand
    years!

On one particular occasion I was moved by a news item about an old man in Bei-tou, Taiwan, who sought the plea-

---

[4] Po Chu-yi (772–846 A.D.) of the T'ang Dynasty (618–906 A.D.) was a high-ranking statesman under the Emperor Hsien-tsung. He eventually became provincial governor of Hangchou and governor of Soochou. His simple but moving poetry won him enormous popularity and lasting fame.

sures of the night. Seeing that the man was old and "tattered," no girl would accommodate him. Finally, after a
long search, he found a sympathetic and unprejudiced girl.
Before leaving her the next morning he presented her with
a check for one million yuan. The check was cashed, and the
young lady gathered her belongings and left Bei-tou. Having abandoned her trade, she was now reported to be operating a restaurant in Taipei. After reading this true story I
composed "The Prostitute of Bei-tou," which appeared in
the *China Daily News* on November 20, 1979:

Duke Huan of the State of Ch'i created prostitution
Thousands of years ago that merchants may ravish on love;
The stars, the moon, the wind and sea are such romantic
    notions
To reminisce upon leaning on the balustrade;
But youth and beauty race against a world of vanity,
And their joy and happiness cannot compare with nature's
    golden sunset.

A man sixty years of age
Sought for that midnight serenade one night;
Soft and tender was the girl who warmly humored him,
Unaware of the reward of a million yuan.
He, after all, was a tattered old man
Who would not allow her to be shamed again with a red
    powdered face.

But love and honor cannot be had for long
When talk is boundless in the kaleidoscope of humankind;
Over words of farewell and flowing tears,
Again and again, in the old brick house, the two exchanged
    adieus;
Then in the morning fog she watched her past fade into the
    mist,
Pondering her new start as the stranger walked away.

# The Lunar New Year

I never mentioned the final FBI visit to my wife, not wanting to worry her. Instead, we began the following week to prepare for the celebration of the Chinese Lunar New Year. It was 4657, the Year of the Boar, and all things would be good and prosperous. Since swine are valuable for their flesh (as pork or ham) as well as for fat (as cooking lard), a family that possessed swine was sure to have plenty of food at its table. In addition, the boar, pronounced "chu" in Chinese, is homonymous with "chu," the precious pearl.

The Chinese language is full of homonyms. The vocabulary of the average person may contain several thousand words, or characters, but there are only a few hundred pronunciations altogether. One distinguishes one word from another through tone and context. The words for boar and pearl happen to have the same pronunciation and tone, so one knows the meaning only from the context. Other words, for example, *ma*, may mean "mother" when pronounced with a high (or what Mandarin calls the "first") tone, or "horse" when pronounced in its low (or "third") tone. Mandarin has only four tones plus a "dropping" neutral tone, which makes it the easiest dialect for foreigners to learn. Cantonese, on the other hand, our native dialect, has as many as thirteen to sixteen tones; foreigners are usually at their most entertaining when learning to speak Cantonese.

Maintaining our Chinese tradition was as important to us as learning about the American tradition. Our Chinese New Year's Eve dinner together would have as much significance as the Thanksgiving holiday, and our New Year's celebration would be as important as the American New Year's Day, the first of January. We were Americans, but we would always be *Chinese* Americans.

The children had no problems living and growing up in a bicultural environment, especially when it came to Chinese New Year! It was always the most joyous of holidays, and it still is. Preparations usually start days in advance. The house is cleaned, the laundry done, and all affairs and petty debts are settled before the close of the current year. Then there is shopping for food and clothing. Everyone has a new outfit for the New Year, and all foods served on that special day are symbolic of good tidings: long noodles for long life; whole chicken for having the whole world at one's command (in Cantonese, the words for "chicken" and "world" are also homonymous, being *gai* and *sai gai* respectively); *fat choi* (a vegetable again homonymous with the Chinese term for prosperity); fish (homonymous with the word for "abundance"); and so forth. The entire dinner has well over a dozen symbolic dishes to last several days past New Year's Day itself, for who wants to cook and work during the first days of the New Year? We Chinese firmly believe that how one starts the year determines how the rest of the year will follow; thus, we relax as much as possible by doing all of the work beforehand! Places of business are likewise shut down so that all employees may observe the occasion in like manner.

The actual celebration traditionally commences with the New Year's Eve dinner. Chinese people for the most part are a superstitious lot, so this particular dinner is always taken together, believing that how we terminate the old year will also be how we start off the new one—in unity, with all family members present. The wearing of something red at the dinner table and the following day is also traditional because the color red symbolizes happiness.

During the course of the meal comes the distribution of the little red envelopes—*lai see* in Cantonese, or "lucky money," as the children like to call it. Even this act is deeply symbolic: It is always the older generation that gives to the younger one, so as to pass on their good fortune to the generations to come. With this money the children get to buy what they wish, rather than what they need. For it is not good to be needy, especially during the New Year holiday!

New Year's Day itself is reserved for relaxation and the exchange of greetings and visits with friends and relatives. Since we always lived in Brooklyn, we had made it a part of our annual tradition to travel to Chinatown for the celebrations. Besides, most of our friends and relatives resided in Chinatown and this was the only way that we could get to see everyone else as well. To the children, of course, visiting meant collecting more lai see, so they were more than enthusiastic about the trip.

But more importantly, we did not want the children to miss out on the traditional Dragon Dance and fireworks. The dragon, we explained to them, is the symbol of China and of all things great and powerful; and the firecrackers are set off to burn and scare away all things evil so that only good things remain for the New Year.

"*Gung hay fat choy! Gung hay fat choy!*" we greeted our friends and relatives gathered in the streets of Chinatown to watch the Dragon Dance. *Gung hay* literally means congratulations, or best wishes, and *fat choi* means to grow in prosperity. That is our way of saying "Happy New Year" to each other, or "May the New Year bring prosperity." Meanwhile, the children happily accepted all of the little red envelopes handed to them, as my wife and I in turn freely gave to the children of our acquaintances. Traditionally, married couples always give two envelopes to each child they encounter since there are two persons to a couple; a widow or widower only gives one. Needless to say, it is always better to have two to give!

Then comes the dragon, dancing through the streets in glorious reds, greens, imperial yellows, silver, and gold! Rolling drums and clashing cymbals announce its imposing presence as storekeepers rush out to catch a whiff of its grandeur.

"Who's the man in the big funny mask?" Wilson asked.

"He is the big-headed Buddha who leads the route for the dragon and directs its path. You see, the people inside the dragon can't see what street they're on, so they follow the man with the mask. He also collects the lai see from the storekeepers as they come out to greet them."

"The dragon dancers get lai see too? I thought only children do."

"Theirs is for good luck. If the dragon comes to your doorstep and you have no lai see to give, then that means you have no luck to give. How can you do business without having a bit of luck?" I explained.

"Oh, I want to be a dragon dancer!" he exclaimed as he watched the dragon parade down the street.

The whole matter is actually a bit more complex than that. For one thing, there is always more than one dragon in any given year, and each one is connected to one of a few major tongs. Each has its own territorial rights, which include the right to collect "protection fees" from its storekeepers. Hence, the lai see they collect is actually a bribe to some degree. While storekeepers would normally give on such an occasion anyway, the tongs demand fees from proprietors doing business on their territories, so the giving is not entirely at one's discretion or free will. If a dragon should accidentally or deliberately wander onto another dragon's territory and collect a fee not rightfully due him, a tong war could start up right then and there. However, these are not the things one tells bright-eyed little boys and girls on New Year's Day.

As the dragon danced along, disappearing down the block, my thoughts drifted back to Sha-tou village in my home province of Guangdong, China, where life was simple and our celebrations were local and free of warfare. From behind the bamboo thickets we lured the dragon to our hideaway, teasing and taunting it along. "Dragon! Dragon! This way!" we took turns shouting. Dazed and confused, it danced toward each child who called to it. Then, just when it was exactly where we wished it to be, we lit the firecrackers and threw them toward the dragon from all directions. It jumped, pounced, and rolled over in the dirt roads of the back country as we pursued it. We surrounded it again, shouting from all sides as before, burning away the evil spirits of the old year with our fireworks, until the dragon died and rose anew with all of its power and glory. What magic we were capable of! To hold the powers of life and death in our hands; to manipulate the forces of good and evil! And when the dragon retired and its players joined in the festivities as mere mortals again, the children carried on the tradition. "I'll be the dragon," the eldest volunteered. "No, I'll be," cried another. "But I know the dance," still another would chime in. And so we played dragon until it was time to feast again.

In the village we celebrated together as one large family. Everyone brought food, and there was always an abundance of it. There was always an abundance of everything during the New Year. If we were too poor to dress and eat properly during the year, this was not to be apparent on this occasion. For this was a New Year. Who knew what the future had in store? On this occasion, we brought out the best of our stock: the most tender of whole chickens and ducks; the leanest portions of beef; the largest pigs, roasted, enough to feed the entire village; the best netting from the sea; the choicest of fruits and vegetables; and the merriest of beverages.

When we sat down to eat we talked only of good things to come. There would be major changes this year: Sha-tou, or "Sand Head" village, would prosper; Gold Mountain men working abroad would send plenty of American dollars home so that we could bring in rich soil, cultivate the land, and always have more than enough food, just like on New Year's Day; every family would have more children to help work the land; lonely Gold Mountain grass widows would find their husbands returning home in style and they would have children the very same year! Young children would grow up to honor and respect their elders, and children coming of age would marry and have families of their own. And even if we knew that certain things might never come true, we said them anyway because it's always lucky to say good things on New Year's Day.

Everyone wore new clothes. In the village where I ran half-naked as a boy, even the poorest of the poor would purchase new clothes for the New Year: pretty red dresses and ribbons for the girls' hair, brightly colored shirts for the boys. For Guangdong, being in the southernmost part of China, was blessed with warm temperatures all year round and very mild winters. Thus boys and girls could freely show off their apparel. What colorful images still ran through my mind! And the voices of laughter resounded still in my head! But the most fashionable display by far was put on by the Gold Mountain wives and their families. They came to dine decked in the finest Hangchou embroidered silk dresses, with matching silk scarves nonchalantly draped across their shoulders. Their displays of fine jewels and gold (sometimes necklaces strung with gold nuggets that they claimed were panned by husbands in Gold Mountain!), made them all the objects of envy and desire. We listened to stories of America—*Mei Guo*, the "beautiful country"— and we dreamed that someday we too would seek and find our fortunes there.

We never heard stories of the laundry men or restaurant workers, or of the tongs and their organized criminal activities, or of the meager living conditions of those trapped in the Chinatown ghettos. We only imagined that if the wives and families left behind by these Gold Mountain men in Sha-tou village were living so well, then how much better off the overseas Chinese must be! Among the many images we pictured were Chinese men in three-piece suits with flowers in their lapels, top hats, gold-rimmed spectacles, and gold-chained time pieces dangling from their pockets, sporting walking sticks for style. But Gold Mountain men rarely returned home; if they did, it was not for long, and they never said a word to us about the hardships, especially not to those who awaited the grand return of a Gold Mountain man decked out in western garb with cigar in hand and pockets that jangled with gold coins. With such great expectations in the air, who dared return to the homeland to dash these hopes? And would they have been believed?

Yet with all of the disillusionment and broken dreams, I could not help but believe that I had made the right choice in coming to settle in Gold Mountain. No, life has not been easy, to say the least, but as I stand here on Gold Mountain soil I do see the stability of life and the secure futures for my son and daughter that could never have been back in China. Yes, this is where we will remain. This is the land of opportunity indeed, and despite the trials and tribulations of McCarthyism I have come out victorious in the end and am my own free person again.

"Father! Father! I am cold! Can we go somewhere warm to eat?" my daughter cried.

"Of course, of course," I answered, not realizing that I had drifted back forty years to another place and time, and to an altogether different way of life. As we sat down for dim sum at our favorite teahouse, I found myself surrounded by a family happy and well provided for, amidst talk and laughter that surely would ring in better years to come. As if awakening from a trance, it suddenly dawned on me that I had indeed struck it rich in Gold Mountain!

# Living in the Present

I am now retired from laundry work, retired since 1978. I did not make much money in the decade before retirement; the newer permanent press fabrics put many of us out of work, so laundry men were already a disappearing breed. But the Chinese Hand Laundry Alliance still exists to help those who continue to come to Gold Mountain in search of a better life. And yes, the myth of finding streets paved with gold still exists too; one need only look to the ever-crowded streets of New York's Chinatown to see the impact of the immigrant dream.

I return on various occasions to the CHLA, mostly to anniversary reunions. I enjoy the fellowship even though I no longer need the services. In my own way I can now look back and reminisce on the "good old days" without the fear of persecution.

Much of my time is spent improving my English, a lifelong endeavor. I would like to recall the story of my life in English one day so that the American public will not forget the turmoil of the McCarthy era, so that all those who suffered will not have suffered in vain. Still I write my poetry in Chinese and publish in various Chinese papers—the number of which has grown tremendously, reflecting the ever-changing needs of the growing and diverse influx of Asian immigrants. One day in the summer of 1980 I read an interesting column in the *China Daily News*—still my favorite paper—written by a certain Mr. Ma. After thirty years in Gold Mountain, he was ready to retire but could not help comparing his life of hardship here with the more leisurely pace of life of the Chinese countryside. My response to him was written in verse, addressed and dedicated "To Mr. Ma at his Retirement":

> You came to Gold Mountain to seek your fortune;
> Now, do not compare life with that in China.
> Neither look back in your golden years with any regret,
> But embrace the twilight after sunset.

An open letter from Mr. Ma in response to the publication of this poem appeared on August 28, 1980, in the *China Daily News*. A translation of it reads as follows:

> On August 16, 1980, in the Art and Nature section of the China Daily News, there appeared a poem written to me by Mr. Lai Bing Chan, the last line of which read, 'Embrace the twilight after sunset.' After repeatedly reciting this line, I now feel that I comprehensively understand your words of earnest encouragement. I have posted your poem in my study as a constant reminder of your good thought, and to encourage myself from time to time to self-education.
>
> Rightly, in the past thirty years, I have been wading through the hardships of Chinese-American society and am now dragging myself toward the road of retirement. In secret I have vowed to myself that during this short span of time I shall read some books and write something. If what I write can somehow affect and transform the customs and habits of Chinese society in America for the better, or do something to enlighten our great mother country, I would be deeply satisfied.
>
> You, a learned man, can write poems and essays to the point. Indeed you are a man out of the ordinary in this Chinese community. I, an unlearned, would like to be under your direction and encouragement to go forward.
>
> With boundless gratitude and thankfulness to you, Master Lai.
>
> Ma Tzu

# Postscript

*Winifred C. Chin*

Tung Pok Chin remained active during his retirement, working on this memoir and writing poetry and commentaries on living, mainly for the *China Daily News*. He gladly volunteered to teach English as a Second Language at a senior citizens' center in New York's Chinatown, and dutifully met his classes every Tuesday afternoon until his death.

Since leaving China in 1934, my father never returned to his birthplace, but he did reunite with his younger son from his first marriage after a thirty-seven-year separation. The reunion was set in motion when my maternal grandmother came to the United States in the early 1960s to see her youngest son (whom we still call B7) marry his bride. She brought with her a personal ad from a Hong Kong newspaper. Two young men in their thirties described their father's appearance and personal history in the ad and said they had lost contact with him soon after the summer of 1949 and were now searching for him. My father responded to the ad and reestablished contact with his sons, my half-brothers. After a long and tedious ordeal, just two years before my father's death, the younger son, Lai Wai Yong, a warden at the Hong Kong Clear Water Correctional Facility, and his wife visited America for the first time.

Their tearful reunion had been delayed because the U.S. Consulate in Hong Kong, suspicious that the son would stay in the United States under the sponsorship of his father, refused to issue a visa. Beginning in the 1960s, just as my father foresaw, many Hong Kong residents had applied for exit visas in the hope of leaving before Great Britain handed Hong Kong over to China. A world tour with a stopover in New York was the solution for getting around the strict quota. But my half-brother Wai Yong harbored no such yearnings to remain here and was finally permitted to travel. He realized that he would never have had such a fine career had he come to the United States as a young man seeking the elusive promise of a Gold Mountain life, and he was no longer resentful about lost opportunities in America. When he retired in 1987 at the age of fifty-seven, he and his wife had chosen to remain in Hong Kong.

Many of our other relatives also have chosen to remain, while others emigrated to Canada, Great Britain, or Australia to start new lives. Those still in Hong Kong worry about the next generation growing up under Communist rule. While the Communist regime has agreed not to make any social or economic changes for fifty years following the transfer of power, letters from our relatives express uncertainty and mistrust. Those of my father's generation are too old to be concerned about how they will be affected. It is a predicament for the younger generation, and surely some will come to Gold Mountain—if not as "paper" children then as foreign students, specialists, entrepreneurs, or as stowaways. Although the gold rush days from which Gold Mountain acquired its name are over, the legend lives on.